The People of Buena Ventura

Douglas Butterworth

The People of Buena Ventura

Relocation of Slum Dwellers
in Postrevolutionary Cuba

University of Illinois Press
Urbana   Chicago   London

Library of Congress Cataloging in Publication Data

Butterworth, Douglas, 1930–
   The people of Buena Ventura.

   Bibliography: p.
   Includes index.
   1. Havana—Social conditions. 2. Poor—Cuba—
Havana. 3. Housing—Cuba—Havana. I. Title.
HN210.H33B87   309.1'7291'2   79-11779
ISBN 0-252-00746-8

FOR MY MOTHER AND FATHER

Contents

Acknowledgments

The Ford Foundation gave the original research grant to Oscar Lewis for his research in Cuba and a subsequent grant to Ruth M. Lewis to write up the data. The Center for International Comparative Studies and the Graduate College Research Board, both of the University of Illinois, gave additional financial support to prepare the material for publication.

I am grateful to Ruth M. Lewis for the use of Oscar Lewis' field notes and for her valuable assistance in preparing this manuscript by virtue of her trenchant comments and criticisms, which did much to augment my own analysis and limited field experience in Cuba. Tom Moore helped to organize and analyze materials from Buena Ventura. Moore, a graduate student in anthropology from the New School for Social Research, worked with the data from June, 1971, until August, 1973, but did not, except for brief commentaries, write up any of the materials in this book. I did, however, utilize many of the compilations and analyses he put together. I thank him and his editorial assistant, Mary Anne Guerrero. Sally McBrearty drew the map of Buena Ventura. Marian Brinkerhoff typed the final manuscript. Theodore MacDonald, Jr., prepared the data on the People's Courts. I edited the materials and reduced many of them for publication here.

Terry Butterworth assisted me by editing and typing. I am indebted to John Chance for his suggestions and to him and his wife Julia Hernández de Chance for translating materials. Joan W. Lathrap's comments on the entire manuscript are gratefully acknowledged. I thank Johnetta Pell for comments and Kathleen Fine for typing. Claudia Beck and Nina Díaz Peterson contributed their translation talents to the Buena Ventura materials. I wish to thank Claire

Siegelbaum for conducting interviews and analyzing data from Buena Ventura along with Rafael Rodríguez, who also did a geographical survey of the settlement with the aid of our Cuban student assistants.

I particularly want to express my appreciation to our Cuban student research assistants for their contributions to the study of Buena Ventura: Edilia Ravilero Mateo, Lourdes Portela Lara, Juana Wong Saborit, Enrique Suárez Zarabozo, Juan Rodney Mowett, Rafael Salinas Madrigal, Elsa Barreras López, and Nelson Cabrera Arencibia. Maida Donate and Enrique Vignier also helped with the Buena Ventura fieldwork.

Finally, I wish to express the debt of all of us who worked on the Cuba Project to the residents of Buena Ventura.

Introduction

The aim of this book is to report the results of an investigation of the
lives of former slum dwellers living in the Buena Ventura housing
project built for them by the Cuban revolutionary government on the
outskirts of Havana.[1] The Buena Ventura study is part of a larger
project on Cuba initiated by Oscar Lewis in 1969–70. The general
purpose of the Cuba Project was to take advantage of the unusual
opportunity to study the effects of drastic social, economic, and
political transformations on personal and family life as a result of the
Cuban Revolution of 1959. A specific goal was to observe the mass
organizations and other revolutionary institutions as they functioned a
decade after the triumph of the Revolution and to evaluate the degree
of success or failure in achieving the aims of the Revolution. So far,
three volumes on the Cuba Project have appeared: *Four Men*, *Four
Women*, and *Neighbors*, all with the subtitle *Living the Revolution: An
Oral History of Contemporary Cuba.*

The material in this volume embraces social, economic, and
political aspects of the lives of the residents of the housing project.[2]
The book is organized in three main parts. I first give a background for
the later, more central materials by presenting a portrait of Las Yaguas
(its real name), the slum from which most of the families in Buena
Ventura were resettled. I then discuss the razing of the slum after the
Revolution, the move to Buena Ventura, and the postrevolutionary
economic situation of the families.

In the second part I describe family and social relations in the new
housing project and how these relations differed from those characteristic of Las Yaguas. Finally, I look into the involvement of Buena
Ventura residents in revolutionary organizations and programs.

The data in this volume are designed to present the reader with a view of one segment of the Cuban population undergoing changes in the first decade following the Revolution. I do not intend to generalize these findings beyond the time and place they were gathered.

Background

Oscar Lewis' interest in Cuba began in 1946 when he was visiting lecturer at the University of Havana. During the course of his stay, he and some of his students visited Las Yaguas, the Havana slum, and Melena del Sur, a sugar-mill community southeast of Havana.[3] Except for a brief five-day visit in 1961, he did not return to Cuba until 1968. In February of that year he met with Premier Fidel Castro to discuss the possibility of doing anthropological research in Cuba. He was particularly interested in studying the relocated slum dwellers from Las Yaguas and conducting a study of Melena del Sur. He also wanted to do an extensive study of people representing a cross-section of Cuban society.

Castro invited Lewis to return to Cuba the following year to undertake these and other studies; Lewis agreed if certain basic conditions were guaranteed. These conditions included freedom of investigation, assurance that the government would not harm or punish any of the subjects for cooperating with the study, permission to bring in necessary equipment and supplies and a non-Cuban staff to help maintain confidentiality and independence, and the right to take the findings of the studies out of Cuba without inspection. Although nothing was put in writing, Castro agreed to these conditions. Oscar and Ruth Lewis got clearance from the U.S. State Department, details were worked out with the Cuban government, and they left for Cuba in February, 1969.

In early fall of 1969, Lewis invited me to join the Cuba project. Explaining that his interests and duties as an investigator made it difficult for him to devote sufficient time to the Buena Ventura aspect of the study, he suggested that, considering my previous experience in Mexico and Puerto Rico, my knowledge of Spanish, and our previous working relationship, it would be desirable if I could spend a year in Cuba supervising the Buena Ventura study. I agreed, albeit somewhat reluctantly, since I was committed to teach at the University of Illinois in 1970–71. But I was also excited about the opportunity for research in Castro's Cuba, so I applied for, and was granted, a one-year leave of absence from campus duties.

The Cuban government approved my visit, and I applied to the U.S. State Department for permission to travel to Cuba, since such travel was normally prohibited. Exceptions were made for bona fide scholars desiring to conduct research, and a passport was issued to me in January, 1970, authorizing one round trip to Cuba. I met Lewis in Mexico City toward the end of February to pick up my visa from the Cuban embassy. Lewis and I flew from Mexico City on the afternoon of February 28, arriving in Havana that evening.

Lewis had had a long interest in the poor of Latin America dating from his landmark study of the Mexican village of Tepoztlán (1951). He located a number of Tepoztecans who had migrated to Mexico City, some of whom lived in slumlike dwellings called *vecindades* (1952). He became interested in the life style of these people and formulated his now famous notion of the culture of poverty in 1958. If indeed there was such a subculture, he wanted to learn how it applied to people living in a socialist state. He had written: "On the basis of my limited experience in one socialist country—Cuba—and on the basis of my reading, I am inclined to believe that the culture of poverty does not exist in socialist countries." After briefly reviewing his trips to Cuba in 1946 and 1961, he remarked, "It is my impression that the Castro regime—unlike Marx and Engels—did not write off the so-called lumpen proletariat as an inherently reactionary and antirevolutionary force, but rather saw its revolutionary potential and tried to utilize it."[4]

The question of whether a social revolution might capture the attention of the poorest segments of the population and involve them in its programs and ideology is an intriguing one. Clearly it must do so if it is to be successful in transforming their habits and attitudes and ultimately eliminating the culture of poverty. As with any culture change, one must assume that the culture of poverty can break down only as part of a larger process, but the intensity and depth of the changes in the economic and social order which occur with the establishment of a socialist regime suggest the possibility of rapid changes in behavioral adaptations as well.[5]

The studies of Lewis and myself of poor families in Mexico and Puerto Rico revealed little revolutionary spirit or radical ideology,[6] and there is similarly little evidence of it among their prerevolutionary

Cuban counterparts. Historically, the anarchist, socialist, and communist movements in Cuba have drawn their support from the trade unions, principally among wage laborers in the tobacco and sugar industries and employees of the railroads and port facilities. They had little backing from the unorganized, the unskilled, and the chronically unemployed.[7]

Fidel Castro's Twenty-sixth of July Movement departed from the classical left-wing strategies by making no fundamental appeal to class antagonisms and by building a political base from a cross-section of the Cuban socioeconomic structure. James O'Conner wrote: "The rebellion at first did not set class against class, but out-groups against in-groups, unorganized against organized, men who either did not want or could not acquire access to the public treasury against those who did, constitutionalists against anticonstitutionalists, youth against age, and . . . idealists against pragmatists and opportunists. Segments of each class stood to lose, while others could only gain, from the annihilation of the Batista regime."[8] Thus, when the revolutionary government came to power, it enjoyed support from all socioeconomic levels, but especially from the "enormous and heterogeneous mass of the economically rootless. . . . the unemployed [and] underemployed."[9]

As late as the spring of 1960, a survey of attitudes of urban Cubans gave evidence of continued fervent support for the Castro regime among all major elements of the population, particularly among the lower educational and socioeconomic groups.[10]

However, it would seem that a genuine class struggle was developing as the revolutionary government began putting its programs into effect through the agrarian and urban reforms and the nationalization of industry. The disillusionment of Castro's former bourgeois supporters and their departure from Cuba on a large scale is well known.

By the summer of 1962 the polarization was quite evident, but within the working class Zeitlin found more favorable attitudes toward the Revolution at that time among those who had had a history of unemployment before the Revolution, but no difference according to level of skill. Blacks, in particular, it seems, backed Castro.[11] Certainly many changes took place in the ensuing years, but when Lewis and his staff arrived in Cuba in 1969, the Revolution still enjoyed support from workers who before the Revolution had been economically, socially, and politically marginal.

Methodology

After planning the research, the next task that Oscar Lewis faced was to explain to the young Cuban student assistants (the *equipo*) the purpose of the study and how the research was to be conducted. He spent several weeks explicating the basic concepts of social science to the students. Although the students had previously received no specific training in the social sciences, they had been taught the general purposes of social research in socialist or communist nations.[12]

In the course of, and as part of, the training of the *equipo,* a reconnaissance survey of the seven new housing projects inhabited by the relocated population from Las Yaguas was carried out by Lewis and the students. After the initial survey, it was decided to compare two of the seven settlements, Bolívar and Buena Ventura—Bolívar because it represented a housing project which was said to function rather well, and Buena Ventura because it admittedly had problems. Buena Ventura was selected as the pilot project and was studied over a year. Because of the premature termination of the Cuba Project, we were unable to complete the investigation of Bolívar.[13]

The students who formed the *equipo* of the Cuba Project, five men and five women, ranged in age from nineteen to twenty-five years when they joined the project, and all had at least a secondary school education. Some had gone on to teacher training programs, and two had some university training. All were scholarship students and were members of revolutionary militant organizations, and all but one had participated in the Literacy Campaign of 1961.[14] Their backgrounds, though, were quite dissimilar. One young woman was from a poor family in Oriente Province and took part in the Literacy Campaign in that province after she completed the sixth grade. Afterward she received a scholarship and graduated from the Instituto Pedagógico José Varona. She was one of the five female members of the Lewis team who had previously been picked for a special *equipo* of the Ministry of Education (MINED) to review primary and secondary school operations in Havana. She joined the project in 1969 but took leave early in 1970 because of pregnancy.

Another young woman was also from a poor family from Oriente. Her illiterate father used to make charcoal for a living, and her mother worked as a maid most of her life. The girl celebrated her fifteenth birthday as a *brigadista*[15] in the Literacy Campaign. In 1962 she received a fellowship and eventually also graduated from the Instituto Pedagógico José Varona.

One of the young men on the research team was from Las Villas Province. His family had belonged to the anti-Batista Twenty-sixth of July Movement and had participated in secret meetings, had issued arms and supplies to rebels, and had given refuge to pro-Castro men and women. The youth was forced to leave school because of his family's revolutionary activities. He was sent to Oriente Province as a *brigadista* in 1961, the same year in which his brother, a captain in the revolutionary army, was assassinated by counterrevolutionary agents. The young man was awarded a scholarship to complete his education and graduated from the Instituto Pedagógico.

Another member of the *equipo* was from a middle-class family in the province of Camagüey. Shortly before the Revolution, his father was arrested and tortured as a political prisoner. The boy joined the Literacy Campaign, later became a scholarship student, and graduated from the Instituto Pedagógico.

Aside from their somewhat similar educational backgrounds and status as members of a special MINED *equipo,* the common bond of the student members of the Cuba Project was their participation as *brigadistas* in the 1961 Literacy Campaign. As youngsters of eleven to fifteen years they were sent to some of the most rugged parts of the island. They had virtually no experience away from home and were asked to undergo tremendous hardships for a campaign which many of them doubtless only dimly understood.

The experiences of these young men and women had shown them what startling changes a revolution with moral and political fervor can bring about almost overnight. These experiences, however, had not prepared them to face the unpleasant reality that a decade of socialism had not cured all the ills of Cuba. This is discussed at more length in a later section of this introduction.

Lewis and his staff prepared a series of questionnaires which were to be administered to each of the one hundred household heads in Buena Ventura. The schedules covered the following topics: (1) a population census, (2) history of occupation and employment, (3) educational history, (4) residence history, (5) *compradazgo* (the godparenthood relationship), (6) a comparison of material possessions before and after the Revolution, (7) felt needs of the residents of Buena Ventura, (8) participation in revolutionary mass organizations, (9) participation in voluntary agricultural labor, (10) general knowledge of Cuban history, politics, geography, and literature, and (11) traits of the culture of poverty in Las Yaguas. This schedule contained seventy-three questions concerning living circumstances in Las Yaguas: housing conditions, marital status, domestic arrangements, education, employment, politics, delinquency and crime, and "life" in the slum. Later, an open-ended questionnaire on social relations was designed. The first questionnaire to be filled out was the basic census schedule (name, age, birthplace, and so on). Ninety-four household heads in Buena Ventura agreed to answer the questionnaire. Two refused the request, and four of the homes were unoccupied at the time of the study. From seventy to eighty-five of the families cooperated in completing the other schedules (except for the open-ended tape-recorded interviews on social relations, which were limited to families with whom the *equipo* had established excellent rapport). Some families simply did not have time to help the *equipo* complete all the schedules; a few became suspicious of the motives of the investigation and discontinued the interviews.

Filling in the questionnaires proved to be more difficult than anticipated. For example, because of the rationing system, the housing shortage, and shifting marital unions, it was next to impossible in some cases to determine just what was the composition of the household. A single ration book was distributed to each household head, in most instances to the person in whose name the house was registered. All members of the household were listed in that ration book, and the household head or his/her representative was the only one authorized to purchase food for the household.[16]

We found, however, that people moved in and out of houses without bothering to change the names in the ration books. Thus, a man who married and moved into his wife's home might continue to eat at the home of his parents because he was in their ration book. Conversely, because of the housing shortage a man might eat meals with his wife (transferring his name to her ration book or perhaps taking food to her home) while sleeping at the home of his parents. In this case, he was officially a member of his wife's household even though he did not sleep there. In view of these circumstances, it became necessary to revise our initial census data to correspond to the realities of household composition in Buena Ventura.

Following the application of the census questionnaire, the staff gathered simple genealogical data from each family. Ninety-three of the families cooperated in this endeavor. The immediate relatives of the household heads were noted along with affinals in and out of the household. The purposes of this procedure were to show marriage and living patterns, check our census data, and help determine kin links in the housing settlement.

During the progress of this part of the research, each member of the *equipo* was assigned selected families in Buena Ventura for intensive interviewing and participant observation. The selection was based, in general, upon the degree of rapport established between the interviewer and the informant. The students' job was to record life histories, conduct open-ended interviews on topics of interest to the study, and record their impressions after each visit.

At first, problems of rapport were formidable, and two of the students were relieved of these responsibilities when they were unable or unwilling to communicate adequately with the families with whom they had been working. I think it is important to note that, although none of the students felt "superior" to their informants, members of the *equipo* were well integrated into the ideology of the Revolution and, in a sense, had been "babied" by the revolutionary regime. They had received fellowships, special rations, and other privileges, and, their experiences as *brigadistas* notwithstanding, had had little or no previous contact with the lumpen proletariat of their nation. One young woman of the *equipo* expressed to us feelings which she seemed to share with the other students:

> We had to prepare ourselves psychologically for the realities we were going to face later on. Those realities were a very tough blow for us. We had a tendency to rationalize all the bad things we saw and resisted recognizing a whole series of social problems which had not been resolved, such as low salaries paid to heads of large families, school dropouts, illicit gambling, prostitution, black marketing, and bearing children just so they can get more rationed goods to sell on the market at inflated prices. The most difficult part was to recognize and tolerate all those evils. This confrontation with reality made us identify even more with the people who lived there. Every day we understood a little more about those who had been despised by society, and now they're going through a very slow process of assimilation into the social norms they must follow, where they'll need the help, understanding, and love that they've always been denied.

Beside this, the residents of Buena Ventura were tired of answering questions government officials had been asking since the early days of the Revolution. People wanted to know why they, rather than some other group, were selected for study. They were reluctant to discuss their past or that of their neighbors. And some thought they were suspected of being *gusanos*—counterrevolutionaries. This last was particularly true when the students attempted to record the material culture of families, since an inventory of items was taken by the Cuban government when a family requested permission to emigrate. A member of our *equipo* related the reactions of people when one of her informants allowed her to ask detailed and sometimes personal questions about every object in the home: "On one occasion, when I was seated on a chair and surrounded by kitchen utensils, a neighbor came in and exclaimed, 'But Alejandra, are you crazy?' This study, in fact, caused quite a commotion in the neighborhood. There were comments like, 'She's investigating every last thing a person has.' And, 'I don't know how Alejandra permits that girl to snoop through her whole house.'"

There were noteworthy differences between research in Cuba and that in other countries in which Oscar Lewis and I had worked. There was always the possibility of government surveillance, eavesdropping, and even intervention—all of which did, in fact, eventually transpire (see Ruth M. Lewis' foreword to *Four Men*). Then there was the suspicion of motives and the problem of establishing some mode of reciprocity between investigator and informant. In working with poor people in other countries, anthropologists have usually been able to help their subjects with regular informant fees or with gifts, medical care, and personal assistance as needs and problems arose.

In Cuba, though, direct payment was not very attractive to informants because there were so few things they could buy with money. Apart from that, direct payment to informants was not advisable because some Cuban government officials felt that material awards of this sort were not consonant with the ideals of the new society. Our Cuban research assistants were also opposed to paying informants and insisted that there should be a purely moral motivation for informants to provide information. In the end we presented our informants with occasional small gifts, unavailable to them in Cuba, brought from the United States.

The workplace of the staff consisted mainly of a two-story building which had formerly been the home of a well-to-do family. After the Revolution the Cuban government had taken over many such residences and had converted them into *albergues,* places of lodging for scholarship students. The Cuban government leased one of these to Lewis for office space as well as for cooking, eating, and occasional sleeping space for the *equipo.* Next door was another house allotted for lodging the non-Cuban staff. That was where I stayed and where I set up my work space. The Lewis residence was located about two miles from our "headquarters."

During the first year of the project, the Cuban research assistants slept in their own widely scattered quarters in Havana, eating only lunch and perhaps a light "buffet" at the office. Later, to save time, some of them began to take their meals there.

Lewis often ate lunch with members of the *equipo* and had them over to his home for dinner and parties. Two, sometimes three, of the students worked regularly at the Lewis home. The students who slept at the office ate breakfast there prepared by one or more of the three cooks, as did an occasional early-arriving secretary. The whole staff—students, secretaries, and I—had lunch together, and some of us ate supper there.

I had been offered the option of taking my meals next door, where I worked and slept, and being served special unrationed food which I was entitled to by virtue of my diplomatic status. However, I elected to eat with the *equipo.* The students had rations somewhat better than the ordinary Cuban citizen, so I was by no means choosing to undergo a hardship. I preferred to eat and chat informally with the members of the *equipo* and the Cuban staff in order to get to know them better and have them know more about me. In any case, the fact of sharing our food was, I am certain, an important reason that the students and I developed an immediate and lasting congeniality.

Lewis and I spent the first few days after my arrival with the *equipo* going over what had been accomplished in Buena Ventura in the year since the project had begun, reviewing problems that had been encountered, and making plans for the future.

The students and I then began a series of trips to the housing project (in a government-supplied van), where I was introduced to the families under study. I never met them all, but I got to know the ones that the students had worked with most closely. I was treated cordially, even warmly, by the families, which demonstrated, among other things, that, after initial difficulties, the *equipo* had done a fine job in establishing rapport with the informants.

The majority of my time in Cuba was spent going over preliminary analyses of the data, interviewing members of the *equipo,* and making recommendations to them about their work. Every Friday evening I held a class of instruction in anthropological field techniques.

In June, 1970, Lewis planned to return briefly to the United States with his family, and I was to be in charge of the project during his absence. The events that transpired at that time have been fully discussed by Ruth M. Lewis in *Four Men.* I shall review them only briefly.

On June 25, the day before Oscar and Ruth Lewis were to leave Cuba, Oscar was requested to appear at the office of Dr. Raúl Roa, the foreign minister. Lewis was notified that the project had been "suspended" by the Cuban government. He was charged, among other things, with accepting funds from the Ford Foundation (something they had known about from the beginning) and studying counterrevolutionary families (which he was entitled to do under the original agreement with Fidel Castro). He was also accused of hiring nonintegrated personnel (secretary-typists), which he had been given special permission to do.

That afternoon, state security agents entered the Lewis home, the office, and the staff home and confiscated all the manuscripts, interviews, tapes, photographs, and personal papers. In total, approximately twenty-five thousand pages of materials, including all the completed questionnaires of the Buena Ventura study, were taken.[17]

Ruth and Oscar Lewis left Cuba a couple of days later, receiving assurances that some of the most important documents would be returned and that they were always welcome back to the island. I stayed on for two more weeks hoping to recover some of the materials, but all I was given upon my departure was a token handful of relatively minor interviews.

As a result of the intervention by Cuban authorities, we had lost crucial data, particularly those relating to changes in life ways before and after the Revolution and to the persistence of a "culture of poverty." This was important, since one of the organizing themes of the Cuba Project was the concept of the culture of poverty.

At the conclusion of the Cuba Project, the materials from Buena Ventura that we had to work with were 7,194 transcribed pages from taped interviews plus 728 pages of impressions and observations by the staff. There were also 93 transcribed pages of materials about Buena

Ventura from taped interviews with government officials and 759 pages of transcripts, interviews, and impressions about the People's Courts. Oscar Lewis died in December, 1970, and Ruth M. Lewis became director of the project.

Shortly after my return to Urbana, I began analyzing the materials and organizing the Buena Ventura data. When I had to resume teaching duties and became involved in another research project, Ruth Lewis turned the materials over to Tom Moore to continue the organization and analysis. When Moore left in 1973, I agreed to write up the materials for publication.

The Culture of Poverty

As mentioned earlier, Oscar Lewis formulated his notion of the culture of poverty after studying poor families in *vecindades* in Mexico City. The basic concept was that under certain conditions in some societies a portion of that society would be so impoverished and lacking in participation in the values and goals of the larger society that it would develop a subculture of its own. As he phrased it initially: "Poverty becomes a dynamic factor which affects participation in the larger national culture and creates a subculture of its own. One can speak of a culture of poverty, for it has its own modalities and distinctive social and psychological consequences for its members. It seems to me that the culture of poverty cuts across regional, rural-urban, and even national boundaries."[18]

The culture (or subculture) of poverty was thus conceived as a design for living shared by many (but not all) poor people and passed on along family lines. As such, it is an adaptation to the conditions of similar socioeconomic environments. Lewis later specified that these settings are class-stratified, highly individuated, capitalistic societies.[19]

Social scientists concerned with the poor have tended to cluster into two camps: those advocating a "situational" approach to poverty, and proponents of the "subcultural" view. Those concepts are not mutually exclusive although the situational position tends to view the behavior of the poor as an adaptive response to a particular exploitative position in which the poor are forced to live, while the subcultural position stresses that, in the process of adapting to an exploitative situation, the poor have developed particular values and concepts resulting in behavior different from that of other segments of society.[20]

Close to one end of the spectrum we find Lewis' formulation of a subculture of poverty, which was picked up and carried to an extreme by Daniel P. Moynihan in the so-called Moynihan Report.[21] The report talked of a "Negro subculture" and the "tangle of pathology" in which most black youth were in danger of being entrapped from one generation to another in "matriarchal" families.

At the other extreme is Valentine's "Ruling Alternative 1" to Lewis' "Ruling Hypothesis 1." The latter is Lewis' basic thesis that the culture of poverty is a subculture with its own structure and rationale. Valentine's alternative is that "The distinctive patterns of social life at the lowest income levels are determined by structural conditions of the larger society beyond the control of low-income people, not by socialization in primary groups committed to a separate design. Otherwise stated, the design for living received by the poor through socialization is not significantly distinct from that of the society as a whole, but the actual conditions of low-income life are importantly inconsistent with actualization of this cultural design."[22]

Using data from his investigation of a squatter settlement in Oaxaca, Mexico, Higgins has shown that these positions are not necessarily contradictory or mutually exclusive.[23] Parker and Kleiner, in their study of black males in Philadelphia, claimed that their data did not support either extreme, but, they argued,

> Negroes living in poverty *are* characterized by a "subculture of poverty" with its modal (but by no means unique) set of attitudes. The behavior of those living in poverty is associated with underlying value positions and is not merely a series of overt reactions forced on them by the constraints of their social situation. On the other hand, our data also suggest that attitudes characterizing this subculture represent but one segment of the total range of attitudes and reference values, many of which are shared with the larger society. Critics of the traditional culture of poverty descriptions are probably correct in pointing out that middle-class social scientists often focus on this narrow range and ignore the wider attitudinal context. However, they are probably wrong in denying that the behavior of individuals in poverty is related to some internalized values.[24]

My own experience is quite in agreement with the position taken by Parker and Kleiner. Surely the socialization of the very poor is distinct from that of other strata, although how significantly would depend upon one's definition of significance and an answer to "significantly for *what*?"

Several critics have noted that Lewis strayed from generally
accepted usage in anthropology in speaking of a culture (and therefore
a subculture as well) having a geographical locus.[25] That does not
seem particularly bothersome to me, since few object to such usages as
a "community of scholars," who may be located in Rome, London,
Berkeley, and elsewhere. Rodman remarked that "if there really are
many similarities among the poor families in the *vecindades* of
Mexico, the rural villages and urban shanty-towns of Trinidad and
Guayana, the *favelas* of Brazil, and the slums and ghettos of Britain
and the United States, then we have really hit upon a fact of major
importance."[26]

Others have pointed out that the concept of culture as a "design for
living" that is passed on along family lines was questioned long before
Lewis' speculation that there could be a subculture within this
framework. It is well known that the intragenerational learning,
particularly among peer groups, is significant to most persons, and that
socialization is an ongoing process throughout one's life. It appears in
this case that Lewis' sin was his use of the terms *culture* and *subculture*
in lieu of something less controversial, such as *cross-cultural type*
or *subvariety*.[27]

Lewis discussed the culture of poverty in terms of economic, social
and psychological, and "other" traits. The economic traits supposedly
characteristic of the culture of poverty include a constant struggle for
survival, work for low wages at a miscellany of unskilled occupations,
child labor, the absence of savings, a chronic shortage of cash, absence
of food reserves in the home, pawning of personal goods, and
borrowing from local money lenders at usurious rates of interest.

Among the most common social and psychological traits are living
in crowded quarters with a lack of privacy, gregariousness, a high
incidence of alcoholism, frequent resort to violence in the settlement of
quarrels, use of physical violence in the training of children, wife
beating, consensual marriages, a high incidence of abandonment of
mothers and children, a trend toward mother-centered families, and a
strong predisposition towards authoritarianism.

Other traits include a belief in male superiority which reaches its
crystallization in the cult of *machismo* and strong feelings of marginality, helplessness, dependency, and alienation.[28]

As with any classification, Lewis' categories may be questioned as
arbitrary. "The entire ordering of traits," commented Leeds, "lacks

conceptualization and logical ordering. In short, it makes no theo-
retical sense."[29] Be that as it may, a more important consideration
is that many of the traits supposedly typical of the culture of poverty
are, in fact, descriptions of poverty. Others, such as alcoholism and
unstable marriages, are probably no more characteristic of the poor
than of other classes.

Insofar as gregariousness and lack of privacy are concerned,
Anthony Leeds has pointed out that lack of privacy is entirely a
function of crowdedness and that gregariousness among the poor is a
function both of crowdedness and of continually mobilizing family,
ritual kin, friends, and neighborhood networks. He adds:

> Gregariousness functions to create communications networks. . . . It
> also necessarily reduces privacy, but privacy, as a characteristic value of
> American middle and upper classes engaged in competition for
> socioeconomic rewards in career structures involving upward mobility,
> may be more or less irrelevant. Privacy is not, as such, a *value* of the
> poor, although . . . the poor [may] explicitly formulate the contexts in
> which they like privacy. However, privacy is a positive *dis*advantage to
> the urban poor, as a large number of them recognized when
> helter-skelter urban renewal, or removal to other residential locations
> without regard to prior community living patterns, broke them away
> from their old neighborhood ties consisting of linked kin and non-kin
> domiciles and friendship networks . . . which operated as mutual
> information and security systems.[30]

I return to this important point later in this work.

Valentine noted that much evidence indicates that families living in
poverty are unconventional in form more often than families in higher
income strata. He maintained that "these statistically unusual family
patterns can generally be traced to externally imposed conditions
impinging on the poor from the society at large. Consensual unions
may be regarded as a flexible adaptation to certain conditions of
poverty. These conditions include fluctuating economic circumstances
which may make it advisable for mates to separate and contract
alternative unions, either temporary or lasting. And female-centered
households may be more functional under conditions of poverty than
'normal' patterns."[31]

Lewis emphasized the multiplicity of relationships between the
culture of poverty (or people living in it) and the larger external system
that generates it. However, as Eames and Goode pointed out, he
frequently confused the two; that is, he included as part of the culture

of the poor aspects of life that are characteristic of the external system, not responses to it. For example, he talked of unemployment as a trait of the culture of poverty, when it is the generator of poverty itself.[32]

Insofar as this study is concerned, it has been mentioned that the culture of poverty was a central concept in the research design for the Cuba Project. Lewis had pretty much assumed that the people in Las Yaguas, or at least a large number of them, had lived in the culture of poverty before the Revolution. He spoke of the "despair, apathy, and hopelessness that are so diagnostic of urban slums in the culture of poverty."[33] As I also mentioned, for verification he included in the schedules to be administered to residents of Buena Ventura questions which he hoped would indicate this prerevolutionary condition, and members of the *equipo* were instructed to keep this aspect of the study continually in mind when taping interviews. The idea, of course, was to determine if people formerly living in a subculture of poverty had, by virtue of the Cuban Revolution, been brought into meaningful participation in the actions and ideals of the larger society. In short, had the "disenfranchised" become a participating citizenry as a result of the events in Cuba between 1959 and 1969?

The question proved to be impossible to answer with any precision. For one thing, because of methodological weaknesses and lack of clarity of the concept itself, we could not even document the case for a culture of poverty in Las Yaguas. Most Las Yaguans had been unemployed at one time or another for varying periods of time in prerevolutionary Cuba, and when they did work, it was in a miscellany of unskilled occupations at low wages. They usually had no savings, and there was a chronic shortage of cash and food resources in their homes. Child labor was usual. Consensual unions were common, and many households were headed by women. Yet, as previously mentioned, most of these traits are merely descriptive of poverty.

Further, the analyses by the *equipo* of the questionnaires about the culture of poverty were inconclusive (the questionnaires themselves were confiscated), the schedules on this subject were dependent upon recall of informants, and the taped interviews which remained in our possession could not lend quantification to any definite conclusions. Oscar Lewis tentatively concluded that about one-third of the families whom he considered to have been living in the culture of poverty in Las Yaguas had, at the time of our study, left it behind them.

Nevertheless, when I turned to the write-up of the materials from Buena Ventura, the conceptual inadequacies of the culture of poverty formulation and the insufficiency of quantifiable data (how does one measure "a strong disposition toward authoritarianism" without at least the administration of some psychological tests?) forced me to abandon the attempt to cast the results of the study in the framework of a culture of poverty.

What remains, then, is a description, unique of its kind, of people living in a strange new environment and their reactions to it a decade after a monumental social and political upheaval. I repeat that the people in this book represent only a small segment of the Cuban population, but perhaps they are similar in many respects to other members of poor or degraded classes of human beings brought up in a neocolonial heritage who are now attempting to define their role in a new society.

Notes

1. Buena Ventura is a pseudonym.

2. Life history materials of some of the families from the housing project and other areas under study were gathered by Oscar Lewis and his staff and organized, analyzed, and published by Ruth M. Lewis and Susan M. Rigdon. See Oscar Lewis, Ruth M. Lewis, and Susan M. Rigdon, *Four Men: Living the Revolution: An Oral History of Contemporary Cuba.* Also see Lewis, Lewis, and Rigdon, *Four Women* and *Neighbors.*

3. For a detailed discussion of the background of the Cuba Project, see Ruth M. Lewis' foreword to *Four Men.*

4. Oscar Lewis, *A Study of Slum Culture: Backgrounds for La Vida*, p. 14. A parallel though somewhat different role of the lumpen proletariat (also noted by Lewis) was made by Franz Fanon based on his experience in the Algerian struggle for independence. He wrote, "It is within this mass of humanity, this people of the shanty towns, at the core of the lumpen proletariat, that the rebellion will find its urban spearhead. For the lumpen proletariat, that horde of starving men, uprooted from their tribe and from their clan, constitutes one of the most spontaneous and most radically revolutionary forces of a colonized people" (Fanon, *The Wretched of the Earth* [New York: Grove Press, 1963], p. 45).

5. I am indebted to Tom Moore for his comments on this point. Erik Allardt wrote: "By definition, the concept of 'revolution' indicates changes in the human environment. One may ask, however, what kind of changes revolutions actually bring about. . . . Revolutions are regarded not only as influencing social structure but also as causing cultural change. The relationship between revolutions and cultural change is, however, an intricate one. The problem is not entirely empirical, but has many difficult conceptual aspects, as we can see most readily by focusing on revolutions in the making, specifically, revolutionary ideologies. Ideology can be regarded as a system of evaluative principles about the ends of human action, about the means of attaining those ends, and about the nature of social and physical reality. To say that an ideology is revolutionary implies a redefinition of ends, means, and the nature of reality. It follows that a revolutionary ideology, by definition is to a certain extent building and creating culture as it is usually defined" (Allardt, "Revolutionary Ideologies as Agents of Cultural and Structural Change," in *Social Science and the*

New Societies: Problems in Cross-Cultural Research and Theory Building, ed. Nancy Hammond, p. 149).

In his *Peasant Wars of the Twentieth Century,* Eric R. Wolf talks of viewing revolutions and rebellions "in terms of a concrete historical experience which lives on in the present and continues to determine its shape and meaning. Everywhere, this historical experience bears the stigmata of trauma and strife, of interference and rupture with the past, as well as the boon of continuity, of successful adaptation and adjustment—engrams of events not easily erased and often only latent in the cultural memory until some greater event serves to draw them forth again" (p. 276).

6. Since 1960 I had been working with peasants from a village in the state of Oaxaca, Mexico, and their relatives who had migrated from there to Mexico City and other urban centers in Mexico. I was research assistant to Lewis in Puerto Rico and New York in 1963–64.

7. Victor Alba, *Historia del movimiento obrero en América Latina* (México: Libreros Mexicanos Unidos, 1964); Robert J. Alexander, *Communism in Latin America* (New Brunswick, N.J.: Rutgers University Press, 1957).

8. James O'Conner, *The Origins of Socialism in Cuba.*

9. Boris Goldenberg, *The Cuban Revolution and Latin America* (New York: Frederich A. Praeger, 1965).

10. Lloyd A. Free, *Attitudes of the Cuban People Toward the Castro Regime* (Princeton, N.J.: The Institute for International Social Research, 1960), p. 7.

11. Maurice Zeitlin, *Revolutionary Politics and the Cuban Working Class* (Princeton, N.J.: Princeton University Press, 1967), pp. 55–97. Zeitlin's sample was limited to fifty blacks employed in plants and factories in Cuba. Of those blacks 80 percent were favorable toward the Revolution, 8 percent were indecisive, and 12 percent were hostile.

12. In contrast to the Western tradition of "pure" research, socialist countries stress the applicability of research in the social sciences to directed culture change. Linda L. Lubrano, in her recent book *Soviet Sociology of Science,* commented on "the leading role played by the Communist Party in the political management of scientific research and development." She tells how one Soviet author concluded that the Communist party and Soviet government are expected to "create and perfect a new type of social organization of science" (quoted by Yakov M. Rabkin in his review in *Science* 197 [August, 1977]: 856).

Scientific research in Western nations is, of course, not always "pure," nor could it be. J. D. Bernal, in a famous treatise published almost forty years ago, observed that "there are . . . two sharply distinct points of view which might be called the ideal and the realist pictures of science. In the first picture science appears as concerned only with the discovery and contemplation of truth; its function, as distinct from that of mythical cosmologies, is to build up a world picture that fits the facts of experience. If it is also of practical utility, so much the better, as long as its true purpose is not lost. In the second picture utility predominates; truth appears as a means for useful action and can be tested only by such action" (Bernal, *The Social Function of Science,* p. 4).

13. Although a community study was not done, interviews with residents suggest that, despite its presumed integration, Bolívar had a number of the same problems as Buena Ventura. We can only speculate why Lewis selected Buena Ventura for the initial study.

14. See chapter 6.

15. A member of the Literacy Brigade (see chapter 6).

16. In most cases, the determination of head of household was unambiguous. This was most obvious when a man or woman lived alone or when one or the other was a

single parent living with his/her children, grandchildren, and so on. (See chapter 1 for household composition in Buena Ventura.) In some cases, though, the assignment of household head status was ambiguous, even arbitrary, depending upon in whose name the house was registered, listings in the ration book, and other criteria.

17. We had copies of about half of those materials in Urbana. Lewis had made seven trips to the United States, and Ruth M. Lewis two, each time taking with them tapes, typed interviews, and copies of everything except charts and questionnaires. This was part of the agreement about freedom of research; not once was a suitcase or other parcel opened for inspection upon leaving.

18. Lewis, *Study of Slum Culture*, p. 387.

19. *Ibid.*, p. 5.

20. For a thorough discussion of different models of à culture or situation of poverty, see Michael Higgins, "Somos Gente Humilde: An Ethnography of a Poor Urban Colonia" (Ph.D. diss., University of Illinois, Urbana, 1974).

21. U.S. Department of Labor, Office of Policy Planning and Research, *The Negro Family: The Case for National Action*.

22. Charles A. Valentine, *Culture and Poverty: Critique and Counter-Proposals*, p. 129.

23. Higgins, "Somos Gente Humilde," pp. 392–96.

24. Seymour Parker and Robert J. Kleiner, "The Culture of Poverty: An Adjustive Dimension," *American Anthropologist* 72, no. 3 (1970): 525.

25. Edwin Eames and Judith Granich Goode, *Anthropology of the City: An Introduction to Urban Anthropology*, pp. 309–10; Anthony Leeds, "The Concept of the 'Culture of Poverty': Conceptual, Logical, and Empirical Problems, with Perspectives from Brazil and Peru," in *The Culture of Poverty: A Critique*, ed. Eleanor Burke Leacock (New York: Simon and Schuster, 1971), pp. 226–27.

26. Hyman Rodman, *Lower-Class Families: The Culture of Poverty in Negro Trinidad*, p. 5. Eames and Goode, *Anthropology of the City*, p. 306, observed that Lewis saw the culture of poverty as a response to *industrial capitalism* and not to the urban milieu. He did not imply that the nature of the city influenced the development of the culture of poverty. But many others have assumed that since Lewis' later work was done in urban areas, he implied that poverty and the culture of poverty were urban phenomena.

27. James A. Ford noted that "as soon as students of cultural phenomena cease to be satisfied with comparisons of mere qualities of cultural traits and begin also to treat their data quantitatively, it becomes apparent that the basic conceptual tool of cultural research is that of type" (Ford, "On the Concept of Types: The Type Concept Revisited," *American Anthropologist* 56, no. 1 [1954]: 42). But, as Julian H. Steward rejoined, it is not that simple. He distinguished four meanings of "type" and showed that each has special significance to the problem. Steward, "On the Concept of Types: Types of Types," *American Anthropologist* 56, no. 1 (1954): 54.

28. Oscar Lewis, *The Children of Sánchez: Autobiography of a Mexican Family* (New York: Random House, 1961), pp. xxvi–xxvii; Oscar Lewis, "The Culture of Poverty," *Trans-Action* 1, no. 1 (1963): 17.

29. Leeds, "Concept of the 'Culture of Poverty,'" p. 242.

30. *Ibid.*

31. Charles A. Valentine, "The 'Culture of Poverty': Its Scientific Significance and Its Implications for Action," in Leacock, *Culture of Poverty*, pp. 207–208. Consensual unions are, of course, increasingly common among nonpoor families.

32. Eames and Goode, *Anthropology of the City*, p. 308.

33. Lewis, *Study of Slum Culture*, p. 14.

Part I

THE HISTORICAL BACKGROUND AND
MATERIAL CULTURE OF BUENA VENTURA

1

Las Yaguas

Shantytowns and the Depression

During the Great Depression of the late 1920's and 1930's numerous shantytown slum settlements emerged in and around the cities of Cuba. Urban slums existed in Cuba before the depression, but slum conditions in larger cities became worse in the period 1929–34.[1] The economic crisis accelerated migration to cities, and most of the new migrants apparently settled in shantytowns.[2] In Havana and other cities, slum settlements rapidly grew in population and soon became small communities with their own commerce, political organization, and internal stratification. Some of these slums, like Las Yaguas, were to achieve considerable unfavorable notoriety during their thirty-or-more years of existence.[3]

The Great Depression was not the first depression in Cuba; the relatively stable socioeconomic pattern of colonial Cuba had begun to come apart as early as 1868 with the planters' revolt against Spain.[4] During the latter part of the nineteenth and first part of the twentieth centuries, when Cuba entered the world of industrial technology and finance capitalism, farmers and small mill owners vied for survival with those who had the capital required to finance the modern sugar mills (*centrales*). After the Spanish-Cuban-American War of 1898, large North American corporations moved onto the scene, buying up the *centrales* and large tracts of land. The revolution in land tenure resulted in a high concentration of land ownership which left much of the rural population landless or dependent. Some of the displaced population shifted to the cities, adding to a growing urban proletariat.[5]

In the depression years of 1929–34 the situation was desperate throughout Cuba, and rural farm workers and small growers probably suffered more than anyone. The bottom had fallen out of the sugar market, and this time Cuba could not rely on other products as she had in the past. Tobacco had also suffered a severe decline. While there are no statistics on unemployment, unofficial estimates run from about 25 percent[6] to 50 percent[7] in 1933 for the island as a whole. The Commission on Cuban Affairs estimated "roughly and conservatively" that about 60 percent of the Cuban people were living at a submarginal level in 1933.[8]

Thomas relates that in early August, 1933, Cuba presented a "desolate and disconcerting picture." There were serious strikes in Havana. Railway workers were out, and newspapers were shutting down. The bars and cafés were closed for the first time in history. Most shops were shut, and there were few people on the streets. There were no milk or ice deliveries in Havana; the situation in other cities was much the same.[9]

On August 13 of that year the shaky dictatorship of Gerardo Machado fell, throwing an already turbulent Havana into more turmoil. Looting and burning of houses was extensive. At least one thousand were killed, and three hundred houses were sacked.[10]

A Cuban scholar wrote of the times:

> The violent expulsion of the constituted government smashed the principle of authority. For a number of years chaos reigned indomitably throughout the nation. Property rights were under the precarious protection of public security bodies whose unstable organisms were permeated by sectarian politicians who openly tolerated and even joined in the violations in the orgy of libertinism that reigned. In this atmosphere of illegality that rent every institution, the shacks of indigents began to appear, many of them built and equipped with the products of the pillage which culminated in the persecution of those identified with the defeated regime.[11]

Many inhabitants of the shantytowns were "squatters" (*precaristas*) who occupied land without official title. The Havana settlements had colorful names such as La Cueva del Humo (Cave of Smoke), Llega y Pon (Come and Squat), and Las Yaguas. *Yaguas* (sections of bark of the royal palm tree) were often used as construction materials for the shacks of the shantytowns.

The Commission on Cuban Affairs provides this description of the settlements: "There is, however, a great deal more to them than the name ["come and squat"] suggests, for these small villages rapidly take on the pattern of community life. Paths become little streets with names, and the houses have their numbers. Tiny shacks appear as grocery stores displaying a few cans of vegetables, tobacco and a few bananas."[12]

Before the Revolution, the poor in Cuba were truly dispossessed. A large percentage of the total population was made up of peasants, the underemployed, and the unemployed city and slum dwellers. "The most salient characteristics of the poor were their powerlessness and their lack of participation in economic, political, and cultural matters. The only relationships that existed between the poor and the rich were those of a hierarchical subordination of the former to the latter."[13]

Life in Las Yaguas

It was with the invasion of squatters in the early 1930's that an area in Luyanó, a dreary, industrialized sector of East Havana, developed into the settlement which became known as Las Yaguas. Although there were residents in the neighborhood before the depression years, immigration to Las Yaguas peaked in the years 1929–34, as it was to do again in the early and middle 1950's. Las Yaguas claimed some 3,500 inhabitants at the time of the Revolution of 1959.[14] A census conducted by the Ministry of Social Welfare reported 740 families, the majority black, living in Las Yaguas in 1960.[15]

Although no census data are available, informants report that many of the early settlers in Las Yaguas came originally from rural regions of the island. However, it seems that an appreciable number also came from small towns and that, in later years, the migrants were largely urban in origin.[16] Apparently there was often a steplike movement of families from the countryside to a small town and then to one of the Havana *solares* (tenements) before the eventual move to Las Yaguas.

Las Yaguas was an unlikely site for a growing community. Located on an abandoned quarry known as El Blanquizar, its landscape dipped unevenly from a highland bluff to a clay bottom several hundred feet below. A ditch filled with slow-running muddy water bisected the some 6,250 square meters of El Blanquizar. A nearby tobacco processing plant, La Corona Cigar Company, dumped its refuse into the quarry and polluted the stream.

Yet El Blanquizar held a number of attractions for prospective settlers. In contrast to the inner-city *solares*, the abandoned quarry offered ample space for living quarters, and it lay only a short distance from central Havana. The stream might be contaminated, but the water could be boiled for cooking and drinking. Discarded *yaguas*, baling wire, and wood from the tobacco processing factory provided convenient materials for building houses. People who had never before possessed their own home now were "owners"—legally or not. Minerva Ruz tells of how she became a home owner:

> I had passed by Las Yaguas once with my older sister. I saw three or four of those houses and said, "How can those people live like that, without water or anything?" How was I to know that I would end up living there myself! But we owed a year's rent where we were living, so we arranged to get some land in Las Yaguas. We built our home of tree trunks, *yaguas*, and poplar leaves. Those materials were the original "cement" of Las Yaguas. After our house was built it began to sprout!
>
> When we arrived, there were very few houses, but that didn't last long. I don't know why, but poor people were drawn to Las Yaguas like it was a magnet.

As the community grew in size and complexity, three different *barrios* or neighborhoods became distinguishable. La Habana, located on low-lying muddy land near the ditch which ran through the old quarry, became the commercial center of Las Yaguas. Eight grocery stores, several butcher shops and fishmongers, a bakery, a dry goods dealer, pawn shops, kiosks, a charcoal store, restaurants, and numerous stands selling fruits and vegetables, coffee, fritters, candy, and refreshments were all to be found in this *barrio*. Credit was easy to obtain for small purchases. Vendors from the city began to hawk their wares in Las Yaguas and, since prices were cheap, outsiders patronized the shops, bars, and restaurants.

Most of the business enterprises were located along or near the Calle del Medio, main street of La Habana *barrio*. A section known as "Las Cuatro Esquinas" was famous for gambling, drunkenness, and fights.

A fork of the Calle del Medio led uphill to the *barrio* of Guillén. This was the quietest of the three neighborhoods in Las Yaguas, and, since it was also the cleanest, it became the preferred residential district of the community. It was there that a schoolhouse was built by a Catholic church also located on the hill.

Separated from La Habana by the stream, the third *barrio*, known as Matanzas, extended from the marshy land bordering the ditch to the "Loma del Burro" at the top of the quarry. Both Guillén and Matanzas had several rows of houses along the rises, separated by footpaths and narrow streets. Delivery trucks carrying groceries, ice, kerosene, and other goods, as well as an occasional taxi or private car, entered and left the *barrios* by way of the major avenues in the shantytown.

Most houses in Las Yaguas were one-room structures covered by *yaguas*. Some families had made improvements to the construction of their homes by adding sheet metal. Home furnishings were sparse; almost every household had a bed and a dining table—usually the best pieces of furniture in the home—a few chairs, a portable wardrobe, and perhaps a few other pieces. Children ordinarily slept on hammocks made of jute sacks. Most families ate their meals from tin plates or cans using spoons and their fingers; knives and forks were a luxury. Cooking was generally done over wood or charcoal fires.

Almost every home in the slum had an altar adorned with flowers, glasses of water, and other objects for the spiritual benefit of a favorite saint. Religious beliefs and practices in Las Yaguas, particularly among the black population, revolved around a syncretism of Catholicism, *santería*,[17] and spiritism.

Sanitation facilities were absent in Las Yaguas. Most people disposed of their body wastes in tin cans or similar receptacles and emptied them in communal garbage dumps or in the stream. The people bathed and washed clothes in tin basins and the stream.

In the early years the houses were lighted by kerosene lamps, candles, or cooking fires. Eventually much of Las Yaguas was lighted by electricity. However, not many residences had power lines installed by the electric company—it was customary to hook into the officially installed lines and pay the home owners for the service.

Fires were a constant hazard in Las Yaguas. There was little protection for the flimsy huts when a conflagration raced through the slum. Rufina Rodríguez told us how her mother used to spend sleepless nights worrying about the possibility of a fire and, after Rufina had her own home, the horror she felt when one broke out.

> You know how it is. You're asleep and suddenly a voice, "Fire! Fire!" and the *barrio* all aflame. The worst one I remember was on April 2, 1950. It was horrible. It was about 2:00 or 3:00 in the morning. People had sounded the alarm, but I was exhausted and didn't hear it. I was sleeping with my little son when my sister came and knocked on the door. I still didn't hear anything so she broke through the door and shook me awake. The house was on fire and my sister didn't have time to do

anything but rescue my boy. I grabbed my dress—I was naked—and we escaped just as the house collapsed. I had just sold all my bright dresses because I was in mourning for my sister and had about fifty or sixty pesos saved and I had some nice furniture, too. But everything was lost. To this day we never found out how the fire started. Almost the whole *reparto* burned down and one man was killed.

Begging was not uncommon in Las Yaguas, and beggars often took small children along with them in order to collect more money. Manuela la Mexicana related the custom of renting out children to beg in Las Yaguas. Beggars would pay the parents of the child two to four *pesos* a day for the child's assistance.[18] Many parents did not send their youngsters to school because they could not afford to buy the children clothes or shoes or because they needed the economic contributions of the children. Of the children who attended school, many were forced to drop out after a few years because of the economic circumstances of their families. Enrique Cueva recalls:

> Everyone was in the streets looking for a way to scrounge subsistence. Sometime it was 8:00 at night when we came home and nobody had been able to get even a bite to eat. During the day many of the children went begging for food. We tried to find a house where they would give us at least one plate of food, so we could divide it. There was all kinds of food in the grocery store, but not money to buy it. That's the way the majority of us had to live. There's no need to hide it or feel ashamed; the situation was terrible.

The men and women of Las Yaguas engaged in a miscellany of catch-as-catch-can jobs requiring few skills and little or no capital, as is typical of urban poor throughout much of the world. There were can collectors, bottle sellers, car washers, dishwashers, waiters, newspaper vendors, *yaguas* sellers, street cleaners, construction workers, lottery ticket salesmen, watchmen, pushcart vendors, and men who shined shoes. Some persons engaged in various illicit enterprises ranging from thievery to peddling narcotics to running gambling and prostitution houses. Women worked as washerwomen, cooks, domestic servants, tobacco strippers, and vendors. Prostitution, mostly unorganized, was practiced by some women from Las Yaguas, both inside and outside the slum. Our data from sixty-nine families indicate that over two-thirds of the family heads had been unemployed at one time or another during their stay in Las Yaguas.

There were also the "elite" of Las Yaguas—tailors, butchers, shopkeepers, restaurant owners, skilled laborers, bartenders and bar owners, brothel managers, and gambling house operators. Nicolás Salazar relates that some houses had four gambling tables inside and three outside, with four or five people at each table.[19] Even though these elite lived better than their neighbors, they had to share many of the same hardships, and some of these families took up residence outside the slum. It was not unusual for a family to send a young daughter to live with a relative in some other *barrio* to shield her from the unsavory ambience of Las Yaguas. Other girls remembered well the environment in which they grew up. Margarita Iriarte told us:

> There was a lot of vice and corruption in Las Yaguas—a good many prostitutes, pimps, thieves, and *marijuaneros*.
>
> In general, the people who lived there were birds of a feather. If they weren't *marijuaneros*, they were thieves; if not one thing, then another. According to them, those were the easiest ways of earning a living. Other means existed but didn't suit them.
>
> There were brothels all over Las Yaguas,[20] but there wasn't any particular red light zone. Anyone who felt like it set up a house, so there were a lot of pimps, with their long fingernails, nice clothes, and sideburns, living right in the *barrio*.
>
> People used to smoke marijuana on the street corners, and then they'd get into fights or go home and beat their wives—some would even commit murder.

Although reliable census data are not available on household composition, it is clear from surveys we saw by social workers who had been in Las Yaguas and from interviews with our informants that most households in the slum were composed of nuclear or elementary families—a man, woman, and children—or broken families, usually a woman and her children. Extended families residing under a common roof were the exception.

If more living space was needed, household members often had the option of building an addition onto the home, buying or erecting another dwelling in Las Yaguas, or moving out of the slum. Tensions, arguments, and physical violence may have been more often the result of poverty, marital infidelity, gambling, and drinking than of crowded living conditions. Alfonso Cruz reflects on his youth:

> When I was growing up, my life was having my old man come home drunk and my mother not liking it. They argued practically every day. Lots of time my old man would finish work at 11:00 in the morning and come home drunk about 3:00 or 4:00 in the afternoon, although never to the point of passing out or insulting people. He never really got stinking

drunk, but *mamá* didn't like it and it always caused problems. It affected me so much that often I'd quarrel with them and want to leave home. That's the reason I got married so young.

Casual sexual liaisons often resulted in unwanted pregnancies, and, despite some knowledge of primitive abortion techniques, most women carried through their pregnancies. Births took place either in a nearby clinic in Luyanó or at home, often assisted by a midwife from the clinic. Infant mortality was high, partly due to the unsanitary conditions prevailing in the slum.

Most marriages were consensual unions, often of short duration. Legal marriage offered little prestige to a couple within the settlement. Economic circumstances permitting, a man might maintain two households, but in keeping with Latin American tradition there would be a recognized "first wife." This custom is part of the *machismo* complex found at all levels of Cuban society.

On the other hand, a man's authority within the family was frequently limited by his earning power. Women were thus relatively independent and often earned their own money. They had a strong voice in decisions, economic or otherwise, and exerted powerful influence in the Las Yaguas household. Enrique Cueva told us: "My stepfather helped support us, even though he wasn't living there. He'd always bring a few groceries, whatever he could manage to scrounge. He had a trade—he was a mason—but he was out of work and could find only little jobs here and there. My mother took a job as a domestic servant and managed to feed and clothe us."

Certainly a substantial number of households in Las Yaguas could be classified as "female-centered" or matrifocal, a phenomenon commonly reported on in the Caribbean.[21]Families in Las Yaguas shared many other characteristics reported for lower-class families in the Caribbean, particularly among blacks.[22] Rodman's study of husband-wife relations in a community in Trinidad, for instance, shows interesting similarities to accounts by our informants about Las Yaguas. There was, for instance, a reluctance to accept responsibility, especially on the part of men, a casual attitude between the sexes, and a pattern of marital shifting.[23]

The "casual attitude" between the sexes (a term preferable to "marital instability") and the pattern of "marital shifting" are common among poor families in the Caribbean. Consensual unions are, of course, compatible with such a pattern. They, like female-headed households, display great variation in frequency and kind from nation to nation and community to community, but, as noted in the foreword, consensual unions have been widely recognized as a flexible adaptation to certain conditions of poverty, although by no means restricted to poor families.

It has been maintained that lower-class women are more interested in contracting a legal marriage than are men. A reason commonly given for this is the prestige supposedly conferred upon a couple, especially the wife, by virtue of having had their union officially sanctioned by the church and/or state. On questioning, however, it may be found that this reason is merely a verbal response to middle-class expectations. "Better a good livin' than a bad marriage" was a very common saying expressed to Rodman by his informants in Trinidad and is an expression also much used throughout the French, Spanish, and Dutch islands of the West Indies as well as in the British or English-speaking areas.[24] A number of informants from Las Yaguas, usually older men and women, expressed similar feelings.

Probably of more importance than prestige to the woman are the legal advantages entailed in a lawfully recognized union, particularly insofar as property ownership and inheritance are concerned. Actions and attitudes of the people about these matters are, of course, ultimately tied to national laws and policies, even though residents of slums like Las Yaguas might not be fully aware of their existence or content.

If it is, in fact, true that women are more anxious to marry legally than are men, exceptions are commonplace. To name but two in the Caribbean area, many women in Puerto Rican slums studied by Oscar Lewis and myself and a number of female informants from Las Yaguas expressed no desire to legalize their unions because they did not wish to share their property with their spouses and/or spouses' children.

Mixed marriages, more often a white man in union with a black woman, were not uncommmon in Las Yaguas. Such marriages were often frowned upon, particularly by whites. Racism existed within the settlement, and one of its overt manifestations was sexual abuse of blacks by whites. On the other hand, most of the women that men had sex with were black, since the majority of the population was black. In addition, what may have seemed like cases of sexual abuse were, in all probability, instances in which both man and woman were willing partners.[25]

Most of the former residents of Las Yaguas to whom we directed questions about racial discrimination replied that the color of one's skin was of less importance than the stigma of coming from Las Yaguas. And when the survival of the community was at stake, as during a natural disaster or in the face of outside political threats, racism tended to take a back seat.

Las Yaguas was nominally governed by its own mayor, who ruled with the tacit consent of tbe residents and approval of the police. New arrivals had to get the mayor's permission to settle in the shantytown and pay him a fee.

Three men claimed ownership of the lands of Las Yaguas: José María Bouza, Dr. Cosme de la Torriente, and José Guillén, after whom one section of the slum had been named. Already by 1934 they had protested the arrogation of their lands, but they had little success in their attempts to oust the squatters. Finally, in 1939 Cosme de la Torriente petitioned President Laredo Bru to expel the residents of Las Yaguas. He declared that petitions had been submitted for years "for the return of the lands occupied by the *barrio* of indigent people who were residing there with the consent and cooperation of the Sub-Secretary of Health." Cosme de la Torriente's communication recommended that every shack in Las Yaguas be evacuated and burned to the ground.[26]

In 1944 José María Bouza went to court to sue the residents of Las Yaguas for nonpayment of rent. Lacking in legal understanding, representatives of Las Yaguas visited some law students at the University of Havana, appealing for their aid. The students cooperated and found that no one in Las Yaguas could be sued for nonpayment of rent because there were no contracts or documents stating that the land had been rented.[27]

In October, 1944, four days after the inauguration of President Ramón Grau San Martín, a disastrous hurricane struck the Havana area, leaving an estimated forty-five thousand persons homeless and at least twenty-five dead.[28] Informants report that at that time those who claimed to own the Las Yaguas lands convinced government officials that Las Yaguas residents had become infected with contagious diseases as a result of the hurricane's destruction and that the slum should be quarantined from the rest of Havana.

Whether these allegations were true or not, the government did cordon off Las Yaguas and attempt to resettle the residents, but these efforts were resisted by the slum dwellers with the help of university students. Enrique Cueva related:

One day after the hurricane I came home from the market, and workers from the Public Health Ministry were putting up yellow banners on posts saying that the place was infected. They weren't looking for a way to solve our problems, they just wanted to get rid of Las Yaguas.

They wanted to send us to army shelters in Managua [a small town south of Havana] where there wasn't any way to make a living. We were already used to things here and had our own way of life, so we weren't going to be satisfied with that; we wanted a decent place to live, not a concentration camp.

So I, along with some others, rebelled. We tore down the posts and armed ourselves with sticks and knives. They would have to kill us to get us out of there. We built a barricade of rocks and bricks at the entrance and put up pictures of Maceo, Grau, Guiteras, and José Martí, along with the Cuban flag. Then we made a shelter and formed a commission of some of the older men—because they were the most capable. We younger ones weren't chosen, because people were afraid we'd make a mess of things when the authorities came to talk. Everyone was very excited, and they felt the older, more pacific ones, who had more political ability, should be the spokesmen.

A major carrying two pistols appeared in a car and spoke with the commission. After a while he went away saying, "Well, let's see if we can't resolve this problem," and indicated he'd be back soon.

While we waited to see what they would do, we posted guards for the night. Everybody was keeping watch at the foot of the Loma del Burro and at the entrance we had blocked off. About midnight we heard voices. We all fell to the ground. Then we saw a big truck shining a reflector against the barricade. A fat man with a cartridge belt appeared, and another in blue overalls said, "We're from the Federation of University Students. We came to bring milk and oranges for the children here."

So I said, "Wait a minute," and we went to consult with the older men.

"They say they're students."

"Be careful. Make sure it isn't a trick."

"No, they're dressed in civilian clothes, young men in overalls and carrying pistols."

We opened the barricade and they came in. They got off the truck and went to meet the commission. Manolo Castro was the leader of FEU[29] at the time, and he and several others brought weapons and stood guard along with us. With their support we stood up well.

After this, efforts to oust the residents of the slum all but ceased until the revolutionary government razed Las Yaguas in 1963.

The people of Las Yaguas took little interest in, and indeed were hostile to, most postrevolutionary government-sponsored programs ostensibly designed for their own betterment. This was hardly surprising. Since the earliest days of the settlement, government agents had threatened, jailed, and exploited the populace of Las Yaguas and similar slums. Minerva Ruz, who arrived in Las Yaguas in 1931, recalls their plight: "We'd build a house today, and tomorrow the police would come and tear it down. They would sneak in and take their pleasure of the women or beat them. We all adopted the practice of sleeping with cudgels, since the doors of our houses were nothing but henequen sacks."

Police took their cut of every illegal dealing they were aware of—from gambling, theft, bootleg liquor, and narcotics. At one time the chief of police of Havana was said to be in charge of drug traffic in Las Yaguas. Politicians routinely bought votes from the poor slum dwellers. Margarita Iriarte remembered: "At election time people would come to the *barrio* to buy votes. I didn't pay any attention to what went on because I was just a little girl. I just saw the people racing off, saying, 'Now Fulano will give me so much, but Mengano will give me more'"[30]

On several occasions the Cuban government had promised to improve the situation in Las Yaguas by constructing new homes for the residents. Instead, they tore down the old ones without replacing them. When the settlement was threatened in one way or another, the people cooperated spontaneously. The threat of eviction by José Bouza and his colleagues in 1944, the hurricane and subsequent attempt at relocation of the population in 1944–45, and the recurrent fires are examples of events which united the people. García Alonso contends that the people of Las Yaguas were totally lacking in organizing spirit. Yet in addition to their reactions to outside threats there were numerous occasions on which Las Yaguans displayed an "organizing spirit," and some of those are reported by Manuela la Mexicana in García Alonso's book. For example, the residents backed the construction of a school on the Guillén slopes of the *barrio*,[31] and storekeepers and others in Las Yaguas supported a food distribution program sponsored by the FEU.[32]

While the majority of residents may have been politically apathetic, there was at least a nucleus of denizens of Las Yaguas who were

political activists. Minerva Ruz fought against discrimination toward women of Las Yaguas who tried to find regular jobs. She helped
found the CDR[33] in Las Yaguas. Quite obviously her activity con-
tradicts García Alonso's allegation that "to belong to the CDR's
was something humiliating, since their members were judged to be
informers."[34] It is also incongruous that, while García Alonso stated
that none of the women she interviewed belonged to the FMC,[35] one of
the major characters in Manuela's narrative was secretary general
of that organization in Las Yaguas.

Finally, Manuela and Salomé Luz were involved with the Congreso
Femenino (Female Congress) and the Coalición Socialista Demo-
crática (Coalition of Social Democrats) while in Las Yaguas,[36] and
there were two battalions of the Servicio Femenino de Defensa
Civil (Female Civil Defense Service) in the *barrio*.[37]

So, although Las Yaguas residents resembled slum dwellers in many
parts of the Western world in socioeconomic and political respects,
there were also (as in other slums) upwardly mobile and aspiring
members of the barrio who were interested in the welfare of their
community and nation. The life histories of Manuela la Mexicana
(García Alonso, 1968) and Lázaro Benedí (O. Lewis, R. M. Lewis,
and S. M. Rigdon, 1977) exemplify this civil interest in much more
detail than is possible in this brief treatment of Las Yaguas.

Notes

1. Cuban Economic Research Project, *A Study on Cuba*, p. 410.
2. Wyatt MacGaffey and Clifford R. Barnett, *Cuba: Its People, Its Society, Its Culture*, p. 45.
3. Social scientists increasingly draw a discinction between inner-city slums (decaying tenements, *vecindades*, and the like) and mushrooming "owner-built" squatter settlements usually located on the outskirts of cities. See William Mangin, "Latin American Squatter Settlements: A Problem and a Solution," *Latin American Research Review* 2, no 3 (1967): 65–98; and John C. Turner, "Barriers and Channels for Housing Development in Modernizing Countries," *Journal of the American Institute of Planners* 33 (1967): 167–81. Las Yaguas shared some characteristics of each. This work, therefore, will use the terms *slum* and *shantytown* interchangeably with reference to Las Yaguas.
4. Robert Freeman Smith, *Background to Revolution: The Development of Modern Cuba*, p. 9.
5. *Ibid.*, p. 10.
6. Commission on Cuban Affairs, *Problems of the New Cuba: Report of the Commission on Cuban Affairs*.
7. Rene Dumont, *Cuba: Socialism and Development*.
8. It should be noted that large-scale unemployment did not disappear in Cuba after the depression. Dudley Seers et al., *Cuba: The Economic and Social Revolution,*

pp. 12–13, state that there was chronic stagnation in the Cuban economy from the 1920's onward in real per capita income. They observe that from July, 1956, to June, 1957, overt unemployment averaged 16 percent of the labor force, "and this was the best year of the middle of the 1950's."

9. Hugh Thomas, *Cuba:* The Pursuit of Freedom, p. 615.

10. *Ibid.*, p. 628.

11. Juan M. Chailloux Cardona, *Síntesis histórica de la vivienda popular: Los horrores del solar habanero*, pp. 153–54.

12. Commission on Cuban Affairs, *Problems of the New Cuba*, pp. 159–60.

13. José A. Moreno, "From Traditional to Modern Values," *Revolutionary Change in Cuba*, ed. Carmelo Mesa-Lago, p. 475.

14. *Granma Aeekly Review*, April 29, 1973, p. 8. *Granma*, a daily newspaper, and *Granma Weekly Review* are official organs of the Cuban Communist party.

15. Reported in Aida García Alonso, *Manuela la Mexicana*. Aida García Alonso conducted a survey in Las Yaguas in 1963 when the slum was in the process of being razed. A brief summary of the data she collected was published in the introduction to *Manuela la Mexicana*, the life history of a former resident of Las Yaguas.

16. The distinction between rural and urban, difficult to make in any case, is particularly awkward when working with Cuban census data. According to the 1953 national census of Cuba (the last complete census of that nation's population), "urban" refers to localities of 150 or more inhabitants having such services as electricity and medical care.

17. Afro-Cuban religious cult that combines Yoruban and Roman Catholic beliefs and traditions.

18. García Alonso, *Manuel la Mexicana*, p. 209.

19. Oscar Lewis, Ruth M. Lewis, and Susan M. Rigdon, *Four Men: Living the Revolution: An Oral History of Contemporary Cuba*, p. 319.

20. Other informants report that there were only three brothels in Las Yaguas. These, however, were established houses, whereas the ones referred to here might have been "fly-by-night" setups.

21. There is growing body of literature on matrifocality in the Caribbean. The reader is referred particularly to works by González, Martínez-Alier, Rodman, Safa, M. G. Smith, and R. T. Smith listed in the bibliography. Definitions of matrifocality vary. For some scholars, matrifocality means simply the physical absence of the husband/father or other adult male in the household. For others it is defined in terms of distribution of authority. Raymond T. Smith, for example, views matrifocality as a stage in the developmental cycle of the family in which the father/husband, because of his low economic status, becomes a marginal member of the household. M. G. Smith, in contrast, sees the matrifocal family deriving from the lack of intent to establish a stable family in the first place. An excellent summary of the above and other aspects of matrifocality in the Caribbean is in Martínez-Alier, *Marriage, Class and Colour*, pp. 124–30. Our data from Las Yaguas indicate that the "developmental cycle–marginal man" notion explains matrifocality in that *barrio* better than the "lack of intent" idea.

22. Among the sources consulted, works by Ames, González, G. K. Lewis, O. Lewis, MacGaffey and Barnett, Nelson, Rodman, Safa, M. G. Smith, and R. T. Smith, listed in the bibliography, are most pertinent,

23. For Trinidad, Hyman Rodman reports: "The reluctance to accept responsibility . . . is closely related to the general attitude of both sexes that trust and confidence cannot be placed in a spouse. They also share a feeling that any marital relationship is a temporary one, and are always ready to replace an unsuitable spouse. . . . This casual attitude between the sexes, which is held more particularly by the man to-

ward the woman, is closely bound to the whole complex of husband-wife relationships. . . . Separations frequently occur and such an attitude cushions the effect of a separation. . . . Such behavior can aptly be called 'marital-shifting.' Individuals may shift from one relationship to another with the same partner, or they may shift from one partner to another" (Rodman, *Lower-Class Families: The Culture of Poverty in Negro Trinidad*, p. 70).

24. *Ibid.*, p. 64. It is interesting to contrast the findings of Safa, R. T. Smith, O. Lewis, Rodman, and Ames in regard to the prestige of legal marriage. Helen Icken Safa (*The Urban Poor of Puerto Rico: A Study in Development and Inequality*) claims that church ceremonies have high status value among the people of the shantytown she studied. Raymond T. Smith (*The Negro Family in Puerto Rico*) suggests that consensual unions are a symbol of class differentiation and a sign of lower-class status which many families are eager to shed. Rodman (*Lower-Class Families*) and Lewis ("Even the Saints Cry," *Trans-Action* 4, no. 1) take the view presented above, contending that legal marriage has little importance to the poor. Ames says that parents prefer children to contract civil marriages, but approve of common-law arrangements if circumstances demand them.

25. In connection with this, see Alfredo Barrera's story in Oscar Lewis, Ruth M. Lewis, and Susan M. Rigdon, *Four Men: Living the Revolution: An Oral History of Contemporary Cuba*, p. 179.

26. *Granma*, May 13, 1970, p. 2.

27. See Lewis, Lewis, and Rigdon, *Four Me* , p. 58.

28. *New York Times*, October 21, 1944, p. 19.

29. Federacíon Estudiantil Universitaria (Federation of University Students).

30. "Fulano" and "Mengano" are equivalents to the English "So-and-so" or "What's-his-name"

31. García Alonso, *Manuela la Mexicana*, pp. 222–24.

32. Leais, Lewis, and Rigdon, *Four Men*, p. 59.

33. Comités de Defensa de la Revolución (Committees for Defense of the Revolution). See chapter 7.

34. García Alonso, *Manuela la Mexicana*, p. 14.

35. Federación de Mujeres Cubanas (Federation of Cuban Women).

36. García Alonso, *Manuela la Mexicana*, pp. 267–68.

37. *Ibid.*, p. 291.

2

Buena Ventura

Almost immediately following the triumph of the Revolution, the Cuban government moved to bring about housing reform. Fidel Castro expressed concern about housing conditions in Cuba from the beginning of the revolutionary movement. In his famous "History Will Absolve Me" speech, made when he was on trial in 1953 for his role in the assault on Moncada, Castro specified housing as one of the six major problem areas he would take immediate steps to resolve when he came to power. There were, he said, two hundred thousand huts and hovels in Cuba and four hundred thousand families living in cramped barracks and tenements without minimum sanitation facilities. Castro proposed cutting all rents in half, providing tax exemptions on homes inhabited by owners, tripling taxes on rented homes, tearing down the hovels and replacing them with modern multiple-dwelling buildings, and financing housing all over the island on an enormous scale. Everyone, he proclaimed, should own his own home.[1]

The revolutionary government addressed itself to urban housing problems almost immediately after coming to power. In January, 1959, a freeze was declared on evictions from urban housing. In March of the same year the state ordered monthly rents under one hundred pesos reduced by 50 percent; rents from one hundred to two hundred pesos reduced by 40 percent; and rents in excess of two hundred pesos reduced by 30 percent.[2] With the reduction of rents, practically all private building ceased. Government construction of public housing was begun.

Also in January, 1959, the National Institute of Savings and Housing (INAV) was created eventually to replace the national lottery, which had been a form of legalized gambling under prerevolutionary regimes.[3] Under the new plan the government sold bonds, instead of lottery tickets, and awarded cash prizes to owners of bonds which bore the lucky numbers.[4] The revenue from the sale of the bonds was put into a fund to finance new housing.

The Urban Reform Law enacted in October, 1960, declared the right of every family to a decent home and outlined a program for achieving that goal. Private renting of urban housing was forbidden. All tenants were entitled to purchase the house in which they lived at the date on which the law became effective. This was to be done through monthly payments to the government equal to the amount of previous rent. Amortization was to be carried out in no less than five years and no more than twenty, depending on the age of the building. As compensation to property owners, the state would make monthly payments to the landlords in the amount of former rent, up to a maximum of six hundred pesos monthly. The net gain made by the government would be used along with state lottery funds to build new housing. The reform law stated that new dwellings built by the government would be granted to families on the basis of need, with permanent usufruct through monthly payments not exceeding 10 percent of the household income. Eventually, the law stated, the government would, with its own resources, construct new housing for families on a reasonable and permanent basis.[5] Application forms for the proposed new housing were widely circulated at the time the urban reform program was announced.

In carrying out the projected reforms, the government met with such obstacles as problems in planning, financing, and availability of supplies.[6] Nonetheless, construction of public housing was carried out, and in most cases the government did make the payments to the original owners of previously rented homes as promised.

Urban slums were one of the government's initial targets. Representatives of the Social Welfare Agency (Bienestar Social Revolucionario) went to Las Yaguas to survey the situation and conduct inquiries into the "revolutionary calibre" of the inhabitants. Those citizens who were deemed not to possess a "revolutionary orientation" were to be "rehabilitated." Local units of the Federation of Cuban Women and the Committees for the Defense of the Revolution were established within the slum, as they were elsewhere in Cuba.

The reaction of Las Yaguans to these organizations was at first ambivalent. For many, harassed by outsiders for decades, the thought of joining national political groups seemed absurd. Some were barely aware of the political upheaval that culminated in Batista's flight from Cuba and Fidel Castro's triumphant march into Havana. Others who had followed the events were relieved that Batista was gone but were skeptical that the new regime had anything better to offer the Cuban people. And there were those few who fervently embraced the ideals of a new society.

When government officials visited Las Yaguas to notify the people that the slum was to be eradicated and its inhabitants relocated in new low-cost housing, many of the residents viewed the announcement as another in the series of attempts to evict them from the shanty-town without compensation. They thought the proposed housing developments were sheer propaganda until the government began to take action.

Many of the new housing projects were situated in established middle-class residential neighborhoods. When it became known that the buildings under construction would house former slum dwellers, some occupants of residences near the housing projects were less than enthusiastic about their prospective neighbors. In response to opposition, Castro suggested to critics of the projects that if they were not able to live next door to former slum dwellers, they should find someplace else to live.

In distributing the new housing, large families living in substandard housing were generally given priority over newlyweds and others whose needs were considered less urgent.[7] Although there were some charges of arbitrary distribution,[8] it seems clear that many of the neediest families benefited from the reforms. The notorious slum settlements in Cuban cities—Las Yaguas, La Cueva del Humo, and Llega y Pon in Havana; Los Grifos in Santa Clara; and Manza de Gómez in Santiago de Cuba—were eradicated and their residents relocated.

The Settlement of Buena Ventura

Seven housing developments of 100 to 126 units each were built specifically for residents of Las Yaguas. Many Las Yaguans participated in construction of the housing projects. The government took a poll of adults in Las Yaguas to determine who was willing to volunteer to work on the construction projects. The majority of Las Yaguas residents, both men and women, volunteered to participate.

Under the "Self-Help and Mutual Aid Plan"[9] the volunteer workers were given free lunch and dinner and two pesos a day. In addition, they were given credit for the hours they worked which was to apply to the purchase of a new home in one of the developments. The hours were to be converted into monetary units and subtracted from the cost of the home. The remainder of the cost was to be paid in monthly installments computed on the basis of income, but not to exceed 10 percent of household income.[10]

Most of the 740 families in Las Yaguas were relocated to the seven new housing projects. Others received housing through the Urban Reform Office, and a few had left the slum, their whereabouts unknown. By the spring of 1963, the settlement of Las Yaguas was empty.

The Buena Ventura development consisted of one hundred concrete houses arranged in four blocks. It was located in a remote section on the south edge of Havana. The blocks of houses were situated on flat land surrounded on three sides by higher terrain, much of which was vacant land covered with grass and brush. On a rise to the north lived the only immediate neighbors—"middle-class" residents of the same *reparto*.[11] Local shops—a grocery store, a butcher shop, and a bakery—were six to ten blocks away. The *reparto* was on a bus line to the center of Havana, and, as no one in the housing development owned a car, residents took the bus to go to the drugstore, post office, restaurants, bank, or cleaners, all of which were located several miles distant. The nearest taxi stand was a mile away. The elementary school attended by most of the children in Buena Ventura was one-half mile to the north. There were no telephones in the housing development. In cases of emergency, residents used the telephone in a nearby Ministry of Construction office. A polyclinic, dispensing various medical services, was several miles away.

The four blocks of Buena Ventura were separated by paved streets with curbs and sidewalks. At the time of our study, the pavement of the side streets had potholes and deep ruts; the curbs had crumbled, and the sidewalks were cracked and overgrown with weeds. All the houses needed repainting.[12]

Except for two detached two-story buildings containing four units each, all housing units were single-story. The smaller houses were attached by common walls; the larger ones were separate units. Each house had a small front yard and a back yard or patio enclosed by a two-meter-high concrete wall. Most of the front yards were enclosed by homemade wood fences imaginatively decorated with collages of iron bars, perforated sheet-metal strips, or other scrap material.

The houses were essentially alike in floor plan. Each had a living room–dining room, a kitchen, a tiled bathroom with tub and shower, and at least one bedroom. The number of bedrooms ranged from one to four. Floors were of tile or linoleum; interior walls were of plaster painted in colorful pastels. All rooms had windows with aluminum sashes and louvers with no glass panes or screens.

Furniture, to be paid for in monthly installments, was, except for stoves and refrigerators, provided for each home. The furniture consisted of a couch and wicker chairs, beds and mattresses, a dining room table, and coffee or night tables, the number of each (except the couch) depending upon the size of the dwelling. All families had stoves, but only a few owned refrigerators. A sink with running water and a washtub in the patio were provided for each dwelling. All homes had electric power.

The house furnishings, running water, and electricity, and certainly the sturdy dwellings themselves, were all tremendous improvements over what almost every family had had in Las Yaguas.

On the northeast edge of the housing project was a building (called the Social Circle) originally planned as a community center for social and political gatherings and for adult education classes. That purpose for the center, however, was short-lived. Meetings and classes soon lost their initial popularity, and after a destructive hurricane in 1966, three families from outside the *reparto* were "temporarily" relocated in the building. Three years later those families still occupied the building.[13]

To the west of the Social Circle was a small park, enclosed by a low concrete wall, intended to provide residents with a place to sit and relax. The park had a few shade trees, but the walks were overgrown with weeds and the lamps which once illuminated the park at night had long been out of use. Residents rarely used the area as a park. Women hung clothes there to dry, and several men used the area to pasture their goats.

A wide variety of trees and shrubs lined the streets. *Majaguas* (tropical trees of the linden family) lined two streets, and a species of lowland oak had been planted on several other streets. One avenue had Chinese flame trees, which were also found in the park. Several

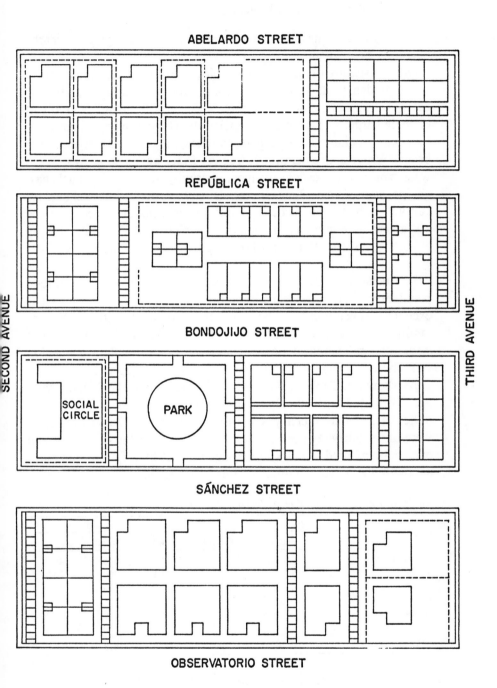

PLAN OF BUENA VENTURA

species of palms, mastics, almonds, chinaberries, and a type of spurge had also been planted.

Most residents of the housing project had in front of their homes small garden plots bright with roses, crotons, marigolds, zinnias, periwinkles, arelias, and shell ginger. Many of the families used part of their gardens to supplement their rations by growing sweet potatoes, taro, manioc, chili peppers, tomatoes, pigeon peas, squash, and beans. Where space permitted, tropical fruits were also grown. There were bananas, avocados, mangos, cherimoyas, anonas, guanabanas, genips, sour oranges, limes, coconuts, and guavas. Additional land for cultivation had been made available to residents at the edge of the settlement as communal garden plots which could be cultivated by anyone in Buena Ventura who staked a claim to them.

In Buena Ventura we studied ninety-four households with a total population of 418. All Buena Ventura residents came from Las Yaguas except for seven families who had exchanged houses with Las Yaguas families, twelve spouses of former Las Yaguans, and the children born since the eradication of Las Yaguas. The Buena Ventura population was characteristically young, nonwhite, and interrelated.

As shown in Table 1, there were 206 males and 212 females, with age distributed fairly evenly by sex, except for a slight preponderance of females under fifteen years. More than half of the 418 residents were under thirty. For reasons not clear, males seventy-five years and over outnumbered females in that age bracket by a four-to-one ratio, although there were only ten cases represented.

Table 1. Age by Sex of Buena Ventura Residents

Age	Males		Females		Total	
	Number	Percentage	Number	Percentage	Number	Percentage
14 and under	75	36.4	93	43.9	168	40.2
15–29	51	24.8	49	23.1	100	23.9
30–44	34	16.5	29	13.7	63	15.1
45–59	19	9.2	22	10.4	41	9.8
60–74	19	9.2	17	8.0	36	8.6
75 and over	8	3.9	2	0.9	10	2.4
Total	206	100.0	212	100.0	418	100.0

Some 42 percent of the Buena Ventura population were black; 25 percent were mulatto, and 33 percent were white. Thus, two-thirds of the inhabitants of the housing development were nonwhite. This ratio of whites to nonwhites contrasted with that of the nation as a whole. According to the 1953 national census, 12.4 percent of the population were black and 14.5 percent mulatto; in other words, only a little more than one-fourth of the Cuban population was nonwhite. The point of this comparison is that it is one indicator that Buena Ventura was by no means a microcosm or representative sample of the nation.

Settling In

Following the eradication of Las Yaguas, the Cuban government sent social workers into the Buena Ventura housing project to help care for the wants and needs of the inhabitants and continue indoctrination lessons begun in Las Yaguas. The workers were not received well at first, but they had good intentions and had the welfare of the people foremost in their minds. They provided medicines, taught the residents hygienic practices, and distributed sewing machines to families who were "clean, well-integrated, and hard working."

Unfortunately, the social workers seeemed to be easily discouraged by failure to rehabilitate the former Las Yaguans in a matter of months. They hampered their own effectiveness by taking recourse to government authorities when unpleasantness arose. For example, two daughters of Sulema Ferrer, who were considered by many to be among the worst reprobates in Buena Ventura, were reported to law enforcement authorities by the social workers—the older daughter for "improprieties" (obscene language and behavior) and the younger for child abuse.

Shortly after the move to the new housing project some person or persons—persumably residents of Buena Ventura—broke into the office of the Social Circle and destroyed files containing confidential information on people in the housing development compiled and kept by the social workers.

One of the social workers told us that the Federation of Cuban Women was afraid to send representatives into Buena Ventura. The social workers took umbrage at this. "We told the Federation a thousand times, 'What's there to be afraid of? Nothing, because the people here are the same as you. They just haven't had the good fortune that you or I have had. But there's nothing to be afraid of.'"

This worker concluded that the myths about the people of Las Yaguas had not died because they made their own discrimination system; that is, they "put down" their own people. For example, she told us, "When we gave a fiesta in the *barrio* [Buena Ventura] their own children said to us, 'Señora, don't invite anybody from here.'"

A feeling of exclusion and neglect was probably the most pervasive sentiment among the residents of Buena Ventura. As mentioned earlier, there were virtually no services within the community, and most "essential" services, aside from the grocery store and bakery, were a good distance away from the *reparto*.

In our analysis of seventy questionnaires about "felt needs" in Buena Ventura, the ten needs most frequently cited were (in order of frequency mentioned): a neighborhood grocery store; a polyclinic in the *reparto*; a shopping center in the *reparto*; drainage and sewage repair; repair of roofs, walls, and gutters; repair of broken pipes; public lighting in streets and in the park; child care centers in the *reparto*; a nearby pharmacy, and a taxi stand in Buena Ventura.

The high priority given to a neighborhood grocery store is of interest since there was one only a few blocks away in the "upper section" of Buena Ventura (the "middle-class" neighborhood). It would appear that the inconvenience of walking a couple of blocks to buy groceries was far less important than the desire of the former Las Yaguans to avoid shopping with their neighbors above.

When these questionnaires were examined from the viewpoint of which needs were listed as first in importance, the order was different, but the list was basically unchanged. Sewage repair was listed by twenty of the seventy respondents as of primary importance. Fourteen informants mentioned a shopping center as their first choice. A dozen mentioned a polyclinic. No more than six respondents agreed on any of the others as first priority. A public telephone in the settlement was mentioned by only four informants as a felt need, and none gave it top priority.

Interestingly, the need for more services and safety outweighed other considerations. Such possible benefits as more scholarships for students, an adult education center, and a closer primary or secondary school were at or near the bottom of the list in both frequency of mention and place of importance. Child care centers—*círculos infantiles* and *jardines*—ranked higher.[14]

Margarita Martínez, a young woman from Buena Ventura, expressed her feelings about the neglect experienced by residents of Buena Ventura:

This *reparto* has always been abandoned. They've regarded it as something apart from everything else, from all other people. At first there was a lot of talk and they helped us cut grass, clean up the neighborhood, and that sort of thing. But afterwards everything was neglected and nobody comes to help us anymore.

Like the houses get soaked inside. Take my house. When it rains, it rains more on the inside than on the outside. Once the plumbing backed up in the house and we got flooded. They came to fix it but what they did was worthless. We kept on getting flooded the same as before. They never fix what they're supposed to fix. The majority of the roofs leak. There's a campaign against gastroenteritis, but they don't realize that kids are sleeping on the living room floor [because of a shortage of beds] and getting drenched because their bedroom is even more flooded. Water runs through the whole house like a river. Nobody can sleep because of the stench and the mosquitos. The people from the upper *reparto* report their problems and they get help. But not us. It's a whole series of things. The garbage truck goes by there, but here we're lucky if it passes by one street, so the garbage just accumulates and accumulates.

Everything's like that. If you have to call a doctor, there's no phone. There's no bus; no cars. Call an ambulance, and if the person is gravely ill he dies because the ambulance doesn't come or maybe it comes at midnight in the middle of a rainstorm and won't come into the *reparto* because the roads are too bad, or they're afraid to enter.

Margarita's observations are not entirely correct or objective, but they do reflect the sentiments of many of the people "down below."

Residents of the "*reparto* above" were ambivalent toward the "people below," but there was by no means uniform rejection by the former. One woman in the upper *reparto* told us:

The only ones who have tried to approach us are those with the most schooling and, above all, those who are the most revolutionary. Nobody here has rejected them.

I think it would have been better to mingle them with groups of educated people so they could be assimilated. They feel marginal and isolated. If they had been placed among decent revolutionary people, they wouldn't steal from each other or cover up for one another. Besides, our revolutionary policy wouldn't permit them to be discriminated against. The organizations of the masses haven't given them the necessary attention. The people down below feel betrayed and defrauded.

Buena Venturans in the housing project were acutely aware of the disdain some of the CDR sectional officials displayed toward them. The wife of the former head of the sectional CDR in charge of Buena Ventura candidly said of the residents of the housing development:

I don't know anything about the people down there. I get sick every time I go to the store and see their scandalous behavior and hear their foul language.

I know some of them by sight, like Raquel Maderas. She's a decent woman, so I don't know how she can stand to live down there.[15] But take that Sulema Ferrer. They ought to burn her along with all her daughters. She goes to the store griping about the food: "There's none of this, there's none of the other," and right in front of everybody she's black-marketing chicken. Those of us who have managed to live halfway decently don't complain, but they spend their life bitching.

And her daughters' kids—those little black ones! They have one every year just to have another naked dirty kid drinking sugar water. That's their custom.

When this informant was asked what had been the reaction of the people "up above" to the move of Las Yaguans into their neighborhood, the woman replied: "Well, just imagine! So many honorable and decent people living here. Naturally, nobody wants them. And now they say they're going to move the people from El Moro here.[16] They're worse than those people down below. We'll just have to move from here."

Her husband, the former president of the sectional CDR, looked more kindly upon the residents of Buena Ventura:

They respect the people here. At first they got into fights and used obscene language, but little by little they've improved. They pass by and say hello to us. And some of them are real revolutionaries. Very few, but there are some. On the other hand, some of them, from the youngest child to the oldest adult, are delinquents. . . . It was a mistake to congregate them all together. It's the same as having them in Las Yaguas, except here they have nice houses. I would have broken them up, putting them with other kinds of people so that social pressure would have made them change.

The only other immediate neighbors of the Buena Venturans were the workers at the Ministry of Construction depot which bordered on the *reparto*. A foreman at the plant told us that he held the residents of the housing project in poor esteem because of their lowly social position. He said there was virtually no interaction between his workers and the people of the housing project. His workers were "middle class," the people of Buena Ventura "lower class." The only interaction which occurred, aside from the occasional use of the depot telephone or an urgent request for a ride to the hospital, was when the girls from the development flirted with depot workers. The foreman deplored what he called "the sexual advances" and "obscene language" of the girls and told us he was going to try to close the street which divided the depot from the housing development. Despite his obvious bias, the foreman admitted that the women who conducted themselves in this manner were a distinct minority.

Many people wanted to leave Buena Ventura to begin a new life elsewhere. One elderly man told us:

> The truth is that I'd like to move from here. I don't agree with the thesis that you should leave the bad caked onto the good, because as soon as you let evil mix with good, everyone is looked upon as the same—bad. There's an old saying that goes, "Tell me who you walk with, and I'll tell you who you are." You may not be bad, but if you go around with shameless people, others will say, "Juana is no better than her sister." It's the same as in Las Yaguas. The only thing that the Revolution has changed is these houses, not the people. It's the same environment. There are ten or twelve people here who give us all a bad reputation. I pointed this out to the *compañera* in charge of clearing out Las Yaguas and other slums. I said to her, "Are you planning to move that bad element into the new *repartos*? You'll never be able to reform them." And a few months after turning over the new housing project to them she said to me, "I remember what you told me, and now I see with my own eyes that it's true." Up the hill they call this Las Yaguas de Mampostería [Las Yaguas made of cement]. That's why I'm trying to get out of here, because this place has a reputation far and wide. And I'm not spreading hearsay—it's the truth. Buena Ventura is Las Yaguas with cement houses, and everybody knows it.

The reputation of old Las Yaguas and the resettled residents in the new housing project had indeed spread far. Perhaps this was most poignantly expressed in the words of a teen-aged girl from Buena Ventura who was teaching school in the Isle of Youth: "I've never told anyone that I had lived in Las Yaguas, and I never will. They'd look upon me as something dirty, something despicable. I have a new life here [on the Isle of Youth] and I don't want any reminders of the past." Most of the young people who spoke of Las Yaguas in that way hardly remembered the old shantytown. They were told of its reputed evils by those who had lived there or by others with nothing more to go on than hearsay. Insofar as the former Las Yaguans are concerned, it might be that those who criticized the old life the most were the very ones who defended it most in the past.

Notes

1. Fidel Castro, *History Will Absolve Me*, pp. 31–34.
2. The Cuban peso remained officially at par with the U.S. dollar after Castro took power.
3. The Castro government allowed the existing lottery to continue for approximately one and one-half years, using the revenue to finance housing construction, and then abolished it.
4. The bonds were "recoverable after five years at 110 percent of cost with annual interest reaching 4 percent after seven years" (*Cuba Review*, Mar., 1975; p. 5). According to Ruby Hart Phillips (*Cuba: Island of Paradox*, p. 53), Cubans would not buy the bonds because the prizes were not attractive enough, nor were people interested in savings. The few people who did purchase the bonds cashed them in immediately rather than leaving them in the savings plan (Cuban Economic Research Project, *A Study on Cuba*, p. 727).
5. Cuba, Instituto Nacional de Reforma Agraria, *Ley de Reforma Agraria*, pp. 4–5.
6. Edward Boorstein, an American economist who worked with Cuban government planning agencies from 1960 to 1963, observed that "the INAV projects reflected American middle-class standards rather than an attempt to meet the needs of a country as poor and short of housing as Cuba. Individual units cost about $8,000–$10,000 and were designed with an abundance of fixtures and gadgets, almost all of them of U.S. manufacture" (*The Economic Transformation of Cuba*, p. 41).
7. Fidel Castro, "Mesa redonda sobre reforma urbana," *Obra Revolucionaria*, June 5, 1962, p. 12.
8. Cuban Economic Research Project, *Study on Cuba*, p. 727.
9. The Plan de Esfuerzo Propio y Ayuda Mutua.
10. *Cuba Review*, March, 1975, p. 6.
11. A *reparto* is geographical unit composed of one or more neighborhoods. *Neighborhood* is a term of no agreed-upon definition in the social sciences but generally suggests a limited area where face-to-face interaction is frequent. *Neighborhood* and *community* are used interchangeably in this work to refer to the Buena Ventura housing project. Informants, however, used the term *reparto* to refer to both the housing project as an isolate and the project plus the adjoining neighborhood. The term *barrio* is used in a similarly loose sense to define a neighborhood.
12. The year 1969–70 was a particularly bad one for Cuba. Almost all materials were in short supply. Moreover, the condition of Buena Ventura was another aspect of the Cuban policy of neglecting urban areas to the preference of rural zones.
13. These families were not included in our survey.
14. The *círculo infantil*, a children's "circle" or nursery school, was part of a nationwide program of child care centers under the jurisdiction of the Federation of Cuban Women. The *círculos* accepted children from forty-five days to five years old. The service, intended primarily for working mothers, had been free since January, 1967. In 1969 there were 44,245 children enrolled in 364 *círculos*, with 30 additional circles under construction. The *jardín* was a nursery school less structured than the *círculo*. In the *jardín*, the children were free to play undirected out-of-doors, usually in a fenced-in park or garden, most of the day. They went home before the evening meal. (*Granma*, July 4, 1969, p. 3) See Marvin Leiner and Robert Ubell, *Children Are the Revolution: Child Care in Cuba*, for a discussion of children's education in Cuba.
15. Raquel Maderos was not from Las Yaguas and moved from Buena Ventura during our study.
16. El Moro was a slum in Havana not far from Buena Ventura.

3

The Economy and Material Culture
of Buena Ventura

The economic activities of the residents of Buena Ventura cannot be understood without reference to the policies of the Castro government. The agrarian reforms of 1959 and 1963, the 1960 law nationalizing 382 major enterprises and banks, and the Great Revolutionary Offensive of 1968, which outlawed small private businesses, meant that 90 percent of the Cuban economy had been taken over from private enterprise by 1969–70. Only in agriculture did a modest share of production still remain in the private sector. Thus, except for small farmers, almost every worker legally employed in the nation was an employee of the state. The labor market and wage structure had been reorganized, and the basis had been laid for the use of social incentives to complement material incentives.[1]

On March 13, 1968, Fidel Castro launched the Great Revolutionary Offensive in a public speech in which he deplored the survival of old institutions and practices, namely, commerce for private enrichment: "Gentlemen, we did not make a Revolution here to establish the right to trade! . . . When will they finally understand that nobody shed his blood here fighting against the tyranny, against mercenaries, against bandits, in order to establish the right for somebody to make two hundred pesos selling rum, or fifty pesos selling fried eggs or omelets, while the girls who work at State enterprises earn the modest salaries, the modest incomes that the present development of our country's economy allows? Who gave them that right?"[2] Castro then announced plans to nationalize retail trade, which included 55,600 small private businesses throughout Cuba. Shops were soon closed, and street vending was prohibited. Private enterprise had become illegal.

Many of the economic activities commonly associated with slums had been largely or completely eliminated in Buena Ventura. Before the Revolution, twenty-five of our male informants had been itinerant peddlers; several had been beggars periodically. None claimed to be engaged in such activities in 1969–70. This change may be seen, on the one hand, as a result of the availability of steady employment by the state and, on the other, as a consequence of the condemnation of private enterprise. Seven women took in laundry, technically illegal, but they were not harassed by local or national officials.

Table 2 indicates the occupational status of the 223 persons in Buena Ventura in the "economically productive" age category of fourteen to sixty-five years. Aside from fifty-eight housewives, who accounted for 26 percent of the group, there were 165 men and women in the category. Of these, 130 (78.8 percent) were employed by the state (including those in obligatory military service) or were students, all of whom were subsidized by the state in one way or another.[3]

Table 2. Occupational Status of Buena Ventura Residents in Age Group Fourteen to Sixty-five Years (1969)

Occupation	Males	Females	Number	Percentage
Employees of the State (nonstudent)	81	18	99	44.4
Military Personnel	11	0	11	4.9
University Students	2	0	2	0.9
High School Students (aged 14–18)	9	9	18	8.1
Housewives	0	58	58	26.0
Self-employed	2	10	12	5.4
Unemployed	10	13	23	10.3
Total	115	108	223	100.0

The two university students received wages at the level they earned in previous employment while they were enrolled in engineering programs at the University of Havana. The two self-employed men in Buena Ventura made candy, carved figures from soap, and manufactured drinking mugs in their homes. If these entrepreneurs had been publicly identified, no doubt they would have been summoned to appear before the People's Courts. The self-employed women—a seamstress, two candy makers, and seven laundresses, worked in their homes. These twelve people were technically outside the law, but no one paid attention to their activities.

Among the twenty-three persons listed as having no occupation, eleven were physically or mentally handicapped. Of the remainder, the five males in the "economically productive" age group who were unemployed included one man who had left his job temporarily for family reasons and four young men, ranging in age from seventeen to twenty-two, who claimed to be seeking employment but were rumored to derive income from drug traffic, black-market activities, theft, or a combination of these.

There were seven unemployed females; that is, women who were single and had neither household responsibilities nor mental or physical infirmities. They preferred not to work and were able to withstand government pressures for women to seek employment.[4]

Not included in Table 2 are four Buena Venturans over sixty-five years of age. The oldest, and the only woman in the group, was a sixty-eight-year-old tobacco stripper. The three employed males over sixty-five were a fumigator, a mason, and a street cleaner. In addition, two elderly male pensioners illegally supplemented their incomes through enterpreneurial activities. One made earrings in his home, and the other repaired and cleaned cooking utensils. Two women over sixty-five took in laundry.

A listing of jobs held by residents of Buena Ventura is provided in Table 3. Despite government training programs, most of the female employees were in the unskilled or service categories. Three exceptions—the seamstress and the two tobacco strippers—had long histories of similar employment antedating the Revolution.

Table 3. Job Description of Employees in Buena Ventura

	Males	Females	Number
Professionals			
Soldiers	2	—	2
Teacher	—	1	1
Subtotal	2	1	3
Skilled or Semiskilled Laborers			
Baker	1	—	1
Butcher	1	—	1
Cook	1	—	1
Assistant cook	1	—	1
Crane operator	1	—	1
Assistant crane operator	1	—	1
Dressmaker	—	1	1
Fisherman	1	—	1
Laboratory assistant	1	—	1
Linotype operator	1	—	1
Machine operators	3	—	3
Assistant machine operator	1	—	1

Table 3. (continued)

	Males	Females	Number
Mason	1	—	1
Mechanics	2	—	2
Assistant mechanic	1	—	1
Office worker (clerical)	1	—	1
Painter	1	—	1
Plumber	1	—	1
Assistant plumber	1	—	1
Rust cutter	1	—	1
Smiths	2	—	2
Solderer	1	—	1
Tobacco strippers	—	2	2
Truck drivers	4	—	4
Subtotal	29	3	32
Unskilled Laborers			
Farm workers	3	2	5
Construction workers	4	—	4
Factory workers	3	2	5
Fumigators	4	—	4
Garbage collectors	2	—	2
Gardeners	2	—	2
Laundry workers	—	2	2
Maintenance worker	1	—	1
Milkman	1	—	1
Night watchmen	2	—	2
Porters	4	—	4
Stevedores	5	—	5
Street cleaners	6	—	6
Subtotal	37	6	43
Service Employees			
Cafeteria worker	1	—	1
Domestic	—	1	1
Newspaper vendor	1	—	1
Institutional attendants	—	5	5
Collector (*recuperador*)	1	—	1
Service station attendant	1	—	1
Store clerks	2	2	4
Subtotal	6	8	14
Details not available	9	—	9
Total state employees	81	18	99

Unskilled and service employees were predominantly men and women over thirty-five years of age. Notable exceptions were the agricultural workers (three men and two women), all of whom were under thirty, and two of the fumigators, brothers aged eighteen and twenty-two, who applied pesticides in the Cordón de la Habana.[5] Their presence in these positions may be seen to be a result of the priority given to the development of the agricultural sector of the Cuban economy at that time. Two of the five institutional attendants worked in nursery schools; the others were nurses' aides in hospitals and in a home for the aged.

The majority of skilled and semiskilled workers were young men who had acquired their skills since the triumph of the Revolution. The main exceptions were found in the more traditional skills such as butcher, cook, and mason, which were held primarily by men over age thirty-five.

After the Revolution a major change took place in the employment of children and young adolescents. Youngsters no longer hawked newspapers, sold lottery tickets, or begged. Because of the limited availability of supplies, minor enterprises such as shining shoes or washing cars were unprofitable. Some of the children in Buena Ventura ran errands for their neighbors in exchange for small amounts of food or money; others, whose families had refrigerators, made sweetened ice cubes for sale in the neighborhood. But remunerative activities for children were much reduced from the scale that was characteristic of Las Yaguas. Child labor was prohibited by law, except for voluntary productive labor (usually agriculture), and school attendance was compulsory (but see chapter 6).

Only one-quarter (25.9 percent) of the Buena Ventura women aged fourteen to sixty-five were gainfully employed outside their homes. In contrast, of the sixty-nine adult female respondents to one of our questionnaires, sixty-three (91.3 percent) reported employment for much of their adult lives before the Revolution.

Since the founding of the Federation of Cuban Women (FMC) in 1960, there had been a very active program to incorporate women into the Cuban labor force. A vast adult education effort including many technical training programs had been launched. Hundreds of nursery schools (*círculos infantiles* and *jardines de infancia*) and boarding schools were established to free mothers of child care in order to work. In addition to slogans, posters, meetings, and radio and television propaganda, in 1969 the Federation of Cuban Women made 396,491 recorded home visits, of which one in every four produced a recruit to the labor force.[6] By the beginning of 1970 the FMC claimed that 113,362 women had been incorporated into the labor force, although not all of them were working at any given time. But the FMC program appears not to have been effective in Buena Ventura.

A major complaint by Buena Ventura mothers who might have wanted to work was that there were no nursery schools in the neighborhood, the nearest being over two miles distant. Yet many Buena Ventura women said that by giving heir husbands steady jobs, the Revolution had made it possible for wives to stay home and devote their time to their homes and families. The Castro government, then, faced another dilemma: how to encourage women to work when they had little incentive to do so.

Rationing

Rationing was introduced by the Cuban government in March, 1962, as an attempt to provide equality of distribution of scarce goods. There were three categories of rationed goods: food, clothing, and non-edible household items. There were variations in the standard rations from province to province and within provinces. The rationing system discussed here is that which was in effect in metropolitan Havana in early 1970.

Food quotas were established on a per capita basis, according to age and health, for all persons officially residing in a household. Some items, such as spaghetti and macaroni, were distributed to household units instead of individuals, and households of five or more members received supplementary quotas for such items as fresh milk.

When our informants were interviewed in early 1970, the quota for rice, the staple in the Cuban diet, was four pounds per capita per month. This amount was raised to six pounds in April, 1970. Many such changes occurred in the apportionment of foodstuffs since the beginning of the rationing system. This was particularly true in the case of tubers—white potatoes, sweet potatoes, cassava, malanga, taro—which were subject to seasonal variations in supply. For example, during a period of abundance, potatoes may have been removed from the rationing system and distributed freely (*por la libre*), or there may have been no potatoes for months. The stipulated quantity of beans was one and one-half pounds per person per month. In actual practice, the quantity was not fixed; beans were distributed according to the amount on hand, whether more or less than the ration.

In metropolitan Havana, individuals were allotted three-quarters of a pound of meat per week and fifteen eggs per month. To augment the skimpy meat allowance and insure a balanced diet, the government was making a concerted effort to encourage the people to eat more fish. However, the best of the fish and shellfish were exported; most fish available to the Cuban people was bony and not very popular. Nevertheless, fish was being eaten more and more.[7]

Special holidays called for additional provisions. On birthdays children (and sometimes adults) were provided with a cake from a state bakery, and a generous ration of beer was provided at the time of a wedding. It had been the custom at Christmas to provide rations of roast pork, a meat virtually unobtainable by the masses. However, there was no Christmas celebration in 1969. It was officially postponed to July 1, 1970, in anticipation of achieving the ten-million-ton sugar harvest.

Infants and children, the aged, the ill, and pregnant women were supposed to have privileged diets. There were also special diets for some workers and institutional employees; scholarship students, children in daycare centers, and people doing military service were fed more and better food than the ordinary citizen. Students and military personnel who boarded at their institutions remained legally registered in their family ration books, as did persons mobilized for agricultural work, hospital patients, and others temporarily absent from the home. Moreover, many industrial and service workers received meals at their work centers without reductions in their quotas.

Yearly quotas were placed on clothing. Minimal annual allowances for men included one pair of leather shoes, two pairs of pants, three pairs of undershirts, four pairs of undershorts, and two shirts. Work shirts were provided free by work centers. Women were entitled to one skirt, one blouse, one dress, two pairs of stockings, four pairs of underpants, and 21½ meters of cloth material. Children on scholarships in boarding schools were given clothing. Distribution of clothing took place twice a year.

Durable consumer goods were allocated according to lists prepared by the Confederation of Cuban Workers (CTC) and other mass organizations. Everyone was given a number which established priority to purchase these goods. Ranking was based upon merits accumulated by the consumer (for example, the title of "Vanguard Worker," the hours of voluntary labor contributed, and so on).[8] The number and types of durable consumer goods already possessed by a family were also taken into consideration.

While the rationing system largely achieved its purpose of egalitarian distribution of goods, it also led to the establishment of a small-scale black market and a great many informal, often illegal, exchanges of goods.

In Buena Ventura, families who could afford to do so purchased all their rations; even if they did not need all of them, they could use the excess for barter or sales. Most trafficking in goods was among friends in the *reparto,* since it was risky to do business with strangers. Some residents of Buena Ventura, however, did not trust their own neighbors and sought trusted partners outside the housing project. Presumably since the women were the ones who usually ran household affairs and often had time on their hands, it was generally they in Buena Ventura who engaged in sales and trade. The majority of exchanges were on an informal and irregular basis, but at least eight homes in the community were recognized as black-market centers conducting exchanges.

Cigarettes were among the most popular items of exchange in the community,[9] but wine and liquor played only a very minor part in black-market exchanges because they were usually unavailable to people except at tourist resorts, where they were sold at exorbitant prices. Beer was available on ration at forty to sixty centavos a bottle. Liquor was illegally distilled and sold in the housing project.

Cash was rarely used in transactions involving foodstuffs, but occasionally it did play a role. For example, at certain times of the month, rice, which normally cost about nineteen centavos a pound, would bring two and one-half or three pesos a pound on the black market. Rice shortages were of particular annoyance to Buena Venturans (and probably to Cubans in general). For a people used to eating rice at almost every meal, except breakfast, the necessity to skimp at meals, skip serving rice at other meals, or do completely without at the end of the ration period was irksome. The slim coffee ration (one and one-half ounces per person per week) was also of special annoyance, as was the black bean ration. The shortage of lard and cooking oil was also keenly felt. The ration of lard had been reduced from three pounds to one pound per household per month, a small quantity for people who do most of their cooking with fats.

Few families owned refrigerators, and perishable foods had to be purchased almost daily. For employed men and women who lived alone this was a genuine hardship, since stores were open only at certain hours, and lines were long. Meat was sold on special days and had to be purchased all at once. Some individuals were forced to rely on friends or neighbors to do their shopping, usually repaying the favor with a share of the rations.[10] This was but one of the strategies worked out by the people to cope with the rationing system. Others included "renting" a space in a neighbor's refrigerator or paying children to wait in line. If someone was away doing agricultural work or military service, he might leave his ration book with a friend who would consume the perishable items and store the rest for the owner.

Families had the option of eating out at government-run restaurants, but meals were expensive, a bus had to be taken from the *reparto,* and sometimes there was up to a three-hour wait to be seated.[11]

The persistence of the long queues is not easy to explain. Certainly there were shortages, but very few of the rationed items were on a "first come, first served" basis. In general, everyone got his fair share, no matter when he did his shopping. In part, the lines resulted from a shortage of store personnel as well as the need for frequent shopping trips due to the lack of refrigeration in the homes. But to a large extent the persistence of the queues seemed to stem from a habit developed when, in the early days of rationing, there often were not enough goods to go around; thus, as soon as people heard of a shipment arriving at the store, they would rush to form long lines and wait until the stock was exhausted. People would join the end of a queue without even knowing what was available.

The lines offered opportunities for gossip, spreading of news, and sometimes good-natured banter, but they were sources of friction, too. Much of the friction resulted from the numbering system whereby a person got a number when he arrived, marking his turn with the persons in front of and behind him. He could leave to go home or run an errand, but he then might return only to find that he had lost his turn and had to start over. Another practice was to have friends get numbers for others, thus saving a trip to the store and the long wait; this was, to be sure, resented by others in line.

Clothing was a particularly popular trade or sale item, and bartering food for clothing was common. In one instance we witnessed, a pair of pants was traded for ten pounds of rice. The trousers were legally priced at four or five pesos, and the rice at about two pesos. On the black market, though, each would have brought twenty to thirty pesos. The trade eliminated the need and risk of cash sale and repurchase.

According to our findings, trade between city and countryside was fairly common and was probably prevalent throughout the island. Farmers had ample food but little clothing, while the reverse was often true in urban centers, since workers got clothing allowances from their place of employment. Thus, through exchanges the imbalance could be righted.

Home manufacturers also played a part in clandestine sales and trade. As previously mentioned, one man earned extra cash by making sweets from his quota of condensed milk. Another man bought empty milk tins from his neighbors and fashioned them into drinking mugs. The mugs were purchased wholesale by a middleman in Buena Ventura who resold them at a profit. Another resident carried on an interesting craft to supplement his pension. He carved figures out of soap in the form of hearts, stars, and flowers, and at the center of each he inserted a snapshot of his customer.

Jewelry was a big item on the black market. In Buena Ventura, earrings were made from copper wire and sold in and out of the *reparto*. The earrings were well made, came in different styles, and brought from five to ten pesos a pair.

Wages and Income

The Cuban wage structure is not clearly understood by outside observers, since the government releases very few statistics. Working from piecemeal sources, Hernández and Mesa-Lago have given us the most coherent exposition of labor organization and wages in contemporary Cuba. Most workers were given quotas, which were based on quantity or time. The quotas specified how many items of a given quality a worker had to produce in a given work schedule (quantity norm) or within how much time a worker had to produce an item of standard quality in a given work schedule (time norm). Thus, a worker had to fulfill the individual work quota corresponding to his job in order to draw the corresponding wage rate from his scale.[12] Workers in the state sector are grouped in four major occupational sectors for wage-scale purposes: agricultural workers, nonagricultural workers, administrative employees, and technicians and executive personnel.

Wages in Cuba in the mid-1960's ranged from a minimum of 64 pesos a month for Grade I (agricultural workers) to about 844 pesos a month for Grade VIII (technical and executive personnel). The *Area Handbook for Cuba* reported that in 1968 the minimum Cuban wage was 85 pesos a month and the maximum was 700 pesos. In 1970 the minimum monthly wage was set at 100 pesos; the maximum was 500 pesos.[13] There were, however, exceptions to this scale, including a provision to honor the "historic wage"—what the worker had been earning before the introduction of the revolutionary government's system.

We compiled data on legal income from eighty-four households containing 365 people in Buena Ventura. The range for individual incomes was from 20 pesos per month (pensioners) to 230 pesos per month (a solderer).[14] The average per capita income was 31.50 pesos per month, or 378.00 pesos a year. This compares with the figure of 415.00 pesos annual per capita income for Cuba as a whole quoted by the *Area Handbook*.[15]

Table 4 shows monthly income of the eighty-four households in Buena Ventura, and Table 5 gives per capita monthly income. Slightly over 40 percent of the households in Buena Ventura had monthly incomes of less than one hundred pesos; nearly one-fifth of all households received less than fifty pesos. These low incomes are largely explained by the presence of a large number of pensioners in Grades I and II.

Table 4. Monthly Incomes of Eighty-four Households in Buena Ventura

Income per Month (pesos)	Number of Households	Percentage of Households
0.00– 49.99	16	19.0
50.00– 99.99	18	21.4
100.00–149.99	17	20.2
150.00–199.99	11	13.1
200.00–249.99	13	15.5
250.00–299.99	3	3.6
300.00–349.99	4	4.8
350.00 or more	2	2.4
Total	84	100.00

The majority of households with gainfully employed members took in from 100 to 250 pesos a month. The mean was 165 pesos a month, and the median was 150 pesos. The high-income households had, without exception, several breadwinners contributing to the household budget.

Table 5 indicates that 69 percent of the households had per capita incomes of under forty pesos while 6 percent earned over one hundred pesos per capita per month.

Income figures mean little, of course, unless we have an idea of expenditures. By taking items available on the food ration and assuming that all these were purchased, we calculated that an adult with no special dietary privileges could live on as little as ten pesos a month for staples. Adding to this non-foodstuffs such as soap, toothpaste, toilet paper, and so forth, one adult could get by on approximately thirteen pesos a month.[16]

Table 5. Per Capita Monthly Incomes of Eighty-four Households in Buena Ventura

Income per Month per Capita . (pesos)	Number of Households	Percentage of Households
0.00–19.99	20	23.8
20.00–39.99	38	45.2
40.00–59.99	9	10.7
60.00–79.99	9	10.7
80.00–99.99	3	3.6
100.00 or more	5	6.0
Total	84	100.00

This amount, to be sure, did not include clothing or any other expenditures; but excluding these items, we estimated that, based on per capita income, only eight of eighty-four families in Buena Ventura could be considered actual cases of deprivation.[17] In fact, we know that no one in the housing project was suffering from hunger. Households with per capita income of less than thirteen pesos per month received aid from friends and relatives, and, as already described, some supplemented their incomes with extralegal activities.

Additional expenditures for families included electricity, transportation, cooking fuel, and entertainment. Estimates for these expenditures made by Susan M. Rigdon for five families in *Neighbors* are as follows: electricity bills ranged from 2 to 10 pesos a month; cooking gas or kerosene averaged 2 to 2.50 pesos per month; transportation cost a minimum of 2 to 3 pesos a month; and entertainment costs—eating out at restaurants or a pizzeria, going to the movies or the amusement park, and so on—varied among those families as they would among any. Our data for Buena Ventura are less specific, but it is clear that almost all families in the housing project had sufficient income to meet basic needs, and many had more money than they could spend on essentials.

The Material Culture of Buena Ventura

One of the objectives of this study was to determine whether the former slum dwellers had bettered their material conditions, apart from improvements in housing and services, since the Revolution. An inventory of selected material possessions was carried out for eighty-five households in Buena Ventura. Seventy-five families in these households had previously lived in the Las Yaguas slum.

Included in this inventory were electrical appliances, sewing machines, furniture, stoves, clocks, and bicycles. (There were no automobiles owned by our informants.) It may be noted that there were no air conditioners in the inventory. Electric fans were therefore prized possessions for Buena Ventura homes, which tended to capture and retain the sweltering Cuban heat. Yet there were only eight fans in the settlement, four of them purchased before the Revolution. The figures from the 1969 survey of Buena Ventura, along with data from the pre-1959 period, are summarized in Table 6.

Comparing the pre- and postrevolutionary periods, the most striking increase was in the number of radios, dining and living room sets, kerosene and alcohol stoves, and electric irons. Conversely, the most notable disappearance was the charcoal stove and charcoal iron, a change largely brought about by electrification (although there were no electric stoves). Only two families in the housing project used more than one kind of stove because of the difficulty of getting certain fuels at different times. A slight increase in the number of clocks was also evident. There were more bicycles than before, although they were used mainly by children.

It was mentioned that all the houses in Buena Ventura were furnished by the state when they were first occupied in 1963. However, we were struck by the fact that six years later, in 1969, only fifty-three of the eighty-five families (64.7 percent) still owned complete living room sets, and only nineteen (22.3 percent) of the bedroom sets had survived intact.

The rapid, severe deterioration of the furniture was the result of generally poor construction and misuse by the families. Beds were particularly in short supply and often in very poor condition. The bed frames were not durable to begin with, and some families did not take much care to preserve them. Many of the mattresses had been rendered unusable by children urinating on them. More important, however, is the fact that many families had grown in size since they were moved

Table 6. Material Possessions of Families by Household (85 Households)

	Before 1959		1969		Increase or Decrease
	Number	Percentage	Number	Percentage	
Electrical Appliances					
Fans	5	5.9	8	9.4	3
Record players	4	4.7	5	5.9	1
Blenders	4	4.7	5	5.9	1
Televisions	5	5.9	3	3.5	−2
Refrigerators	10	11.7	9	10.5	−1
Sewing machines	18	21.1	22	25.8	4
Radios	40	47.1	59	69.4	9
Furniture					
Dining room sets	11	12.9	76	89.4	65
Living room sets	7	8.2	53	64.7	46
Bedroom sets	10	11.7	19	22.3	9
*Stoves**					
Wood	12	14.1	2	2.3	−10
Charcoal	55	64.7	2	2.3	−53
Kerosene	11	12.9	56	65.8	45
Gas	2	2.3	3	3.5	1
Alcohol	18	21.1	39	45.8	21
Electric	1	1.1	—	—	−1
Irons					
Charcoal	56	65.8	2	2.3	−54
Gas	3	3.5	—	—	−3
Electric	21	24.7	67	78.8	46
Clocks	44	51.7	51	60.0	7
Bicycles	11	12.9	18	21.1	7

*Stoves are the only item in the inventory not limited to one per family.

to the settlement, and the government had not been able to furnish them with additional beds to accommodate the increased number of children.

One family had only one bedroom and three beds for the eight members of the household. One of the beds, given to them by a friend, was in extremely poor condition with only a thin mattress covering the metal frame, yet it was used by a married couple, their two-year-old son, and a baby daughter. Also in the bedroom was a crib for the new infant in the family. The third bed was in the dining room where two young brothers slept. A third brother slept on the sofa in the living room.

In summary, our survey indicates that, in addition to better housing and utilities, material living conditions in Buena Ventura and other housing projects had improved greatly since the Revolution. Despite shortages, most former Las Yaguans had more and better clothing than before the Revolution. There was little change in the number of families able to produce expensive electrical appliances. Increase was greatest with regard to moderately priced household items such as radios, kerosene and alcohol stoves, electric irons, and clocks. More people owned more furniture, but deterioration and destruction, particularly of beds, combined with overcrowding had seriously reduced household comforts from the move to Buena Ventura in 1963 to the time of our study six years later.

Notes

1. See James O'Connor, *The Origins of Socialism in Cuba*, for a detailed discussion of the political economy of Cuba during the period under discussion.

2. Martin Kenner and James Petras, eds., *Fidel Castro Speaks*, p. 307.

3. Among the men employed by the state we distinguished between professional soldiers and those performing their duties with the Compulsory Military Service (SMO).

4. The law against loafing (*vagancia*), which provided for disciplinary action against men between the ages of seventeen and sixty and women between seventeen and sixty-five who were physically and mentally fit to work but who did not hold jobs, was not yet in effect at the time of our investigation. It was proposed in October, 1970, passed into legislation in March, 1971, and implemented in April of the same year (*Granma Weekly Review*, March 28, 1971, p. 2).

5. The Cordón de la Habana was a green belt around the city of Havana begun in late 1967 in an unsuccessful attempt to increase the production of coffee and citrus fruits.

6. Nelson Lowry, *Cuba: Measure of a Revolution* (Minneapolis: University of Minnesota Press, 1972), pp. 105–106.

7. One of the most successful revolutionary programs was that of fishing. The output of fish (including shellfish) doubled between 1957 and 1966. In 1968, fish output reached 62,800 metric tons—that is, three times the prerevolutionary output. This total was made possible through an impressive expansion of the Cuban fishing fleet. Carmelo Mesa-Lago, ed., *Revolutionary Change in Cuba*, p. 316.

8. See Carmelo Mesa-Lago and Luc Zephirin, "Central Planning," in Mesa-Lago, *Revolutionary Change in Cuba*, p. 173.

9. Cigarettes could often be purchased legally off the ration at inflated prices. This was part of the attempt by the government to absorb excess cash from the economy.

10. In 1970 the Cuban government began an experimental food distribution system to reduce the time Cubans spent shopping. The *plan jaba*, or shopping-bag plan, allowed families in which adults were working and/or studying to have their shopping done by the employees of the grocery store where they were registered. Workers could leave their shopping bags and ration books at the store in the morning and pick them up on their way home. The system did not go into effect across the island until 1972.

Oscar Lewis, Ruth M. Lewis, and Susan M. Rigdon, *Four Men: Living the Revolution: Oral History Contemporary Cuba*, pp. 138–39.

11. Artificially high restaurant prices were another of the attempts to reduce excess currency in circulation.

12. Roberto E. Hernández and Carmelo Mesa-Lago, "Labor Organization and Wages," in Mesa-Lago, *Revolutionary Change in Cuba*, pp. 224–35.

13. Howard I. Blutstein et al., *Area Handbooc for Cuba*, pp. 130, 361.

14. The minimum pension at the time of our study was supposed to be forty pesos per month. Most of the pensioned individuals in our sample, however, received only twenty pesos a month.

15. Blutstein et al., *Area Handbook for Cuba*, p. 130. This figure would, of course, include such poorly paid laborers as agricultural workers.

16. Oscar Lewis, Ruth M. Lewis, and Susan Rigdon, *Neighbors*.

17. As of 1970, those earning twenty-five pesos a month or less could apply for government assistance and/or exemption from housing payments.

Part II

THE SOCIAL ASPECTS OF BUENA VENTURA

4

Marriage and the Family

Household Structure

The breakdown of family size in the Buena Ventura development is shown in Table 7. Half of the ninety-four housing units studied were occupied by families consisting of two to five persons. Twenty-two homes contained six to nine members, and five dwellings housed twelve to sixteen people. There were twelve two-member households; five contained relatives living together, five were middle-aged or elderly couples, and in two cases friends shared a dwelling. Twenty individuals—sixteen men and four women—lived alone. Most of the single residents were widowed or separated elderly people. Only one was under forty—a twenty-three-year-old man whose wife had recently taken their children with her to live with another man.

Nuclear families (a couple alone or with their children and/or children by previous unions) accounted for only 29.8 percent of all household types in Buena Ventura and composed 32.3 percent of the total population, as seen in Table 8. In contrast, extended families (composed of relatives beyond the nuclear family) occupied 40.4 percent of the homes. As may be seen from Table 9, extended families ranged from one to four generations. The single-generation families were all, of course, extended horizontally and included such kinsmen as cousins and the husband's brother.

The two- three- and four-generation extended families were not only extended vertically, but a number were extended horizontally as well. It will be noted that the three- and four-generation extended families accounted for almost two-thirds of all extended households, and their

Table 7. Buena Ventura Household Composition

Number of Persons per Home	Number of Homes	Percentage of Homes	Total Number of Persons	Percentage of Persons
1	20	21.3	20	4.8
2	12	12.8	24	5.7
3	7	7.4	21	5.0
4	12	12.8	48	11.5
5	16	17.0	80	19.1
6	8	8.5	48	11.5
7	7	7.4	49	11.7
8	4	4.3	32	7.7
9	3	3.2	27	6.5
12	1	1.1	12	2.9
13	2	2.1	26	6.2
15	1	1.1	15	3.6
16	1	1.1	16	3.8
Total	94	100.0*	418	100.0

*Rounded.

Table 8. Buena Ventura Household Structure

Type of Household	Number	Percentage of Households	Total Members	Percentage of Members
Extended families	38	40.4	234	56.0
Nuclear families	28	29.8	135	32.3
Single individuals	20	21.3	20	4.8
Single-parent households	5	5.3	21	5.0
Miscellaneous	3	3.2	8	2.0
Total	94	100.0	418	100.0*

*Rounded.

Table 9. Breakdown of Extended-Family Households

Type of Household	Number	Percentage of Extended Households	Total Members	Percentage of Members
One generation	4	10.5	12	5.0
Two generations	9	23.7	48	20.5
Three generations	22	57.9	138	59.0
Four generations	3	7.9	36	15.4
Total	38	100.0	234	100.0*

*Rounded.

membership included about three-fourths of the total population of extended households.

Single individuals occupied 21.2 percent of the homes, while single-parent families (single women and their children in all our instances) accounted for 5.3 percent of the households. Other types of groupings (for example, friends) occupied the remaining 3.2 percent of the homes.

In thirty-six of the ninety-four households, the house contract was in a woman's name. Twenty-five of these households were headed by a woman with no man present (including the homes of the four women who lived alone), and eleven women called themselves "family heads," even though their husbands resided in the home, because the house contracts were in their names.

The large number of extended-family households was by no means an indication of tight-knit family organization, at least as far as non-blood relatives went. The severe housing shortage in metropolitan Havana made it extremely difficult to acquire living quarters, and relatives were often forced to live together, whether they liked it or not, until independent housing became available. For this reason, the fission in the domestic group which normally would have occurred as children matured, married, and established their own homes often did not take place in Buena Ventura. Instead, when children married, they often had to continue to live in the home of one of their parents. In twenty-two of the thirty-four vertically extended families, married couples lived with parents of one of the partners, and all but two of these families included grandchildren. There were only two cases of married siblings sharing a residence which did not also include a parent.

In addition to internal expansion of the families through births and marriages, household size occasionally increased through incorporation of relatives from outside the neighborhood. Consanguineal kin ties were often strong, so it was generally considered an affront to deny shelter to a kinsman, no matter how inconveniencing it might be to the host. On the other hand, the addition to the food ration book was often welcome, particularly if the guests had "double rations," as did scholarship students (see chapter 3). However, if friction between the kinsmen arose, it was almost impossible to evict the kin-tenants if they were registered in the hosts' ration book.

Several of the above points may be exemplified by the experience of one of our informants, Manolo Romero. Manolo was assigned a home for a single individual when he moved to Buena Ventura. In 1966 he married another Buena Ventura resident, Lorenza Morillo, who brought two sons from previous marriages with her to Manolo's home. Manolo and Lorenza later had a child of their own. In 1968 two of Lorenza's nieces came to Havana from Oriente Province on scholarships. Lorenza persuaded her husband to allow the nieces to join the household. Thus, within five years the original bachelor apartment had expanded from a sole occupant to a family of seven.

There was a complex network of consanguineous and affinal ties which connected many of the families in Buena Ventura.[1] Nearly one-half the households had relatives by blood or marriage living in at least one other household in Buena Ventura. Within this group, no single household was consanguineously related to more than five others; most were related to only one or two others. If we count affinal ties, however, as many as thirteen links among one set of relatives could be traced within the housing development.

The most common type of consanguineous relationship among households was that of siblings. These were most often cases in which couples married and established independent homes in Las Yaguas before coming to Buena Ventura. In addition, many households were connected by parent-child ties, most of which were the result of the child having left the parent's home after coming to Buena Ventura and having settled in the home of the spouse's parents within the housing development.

Courtship and Marriage

Young men in Buena Ventura generally had greater freedom than girls, in the sense that boys could leave the *reparto* more or less at will, while girls were usually more curtailed in their movements. It was anticipated that boys, though not encouraged by parents or other elders, would enrage in sexual activity by pubescence or earlier. Their sexual experiments were usually looked upon with indulgence. Young men were often introduced to sex by an older woman from Buena Ventura or elsewhere. Lip service was paid by residents in the housing project to girls' virginity, but interviews and life histories suggest that it was, at least after the middle teens, often honored in the breach.

During courtship the young couple would meet, often surreptitiously, in the *reparto*. This was somewhat more difficult in Buena

Ventura than it had been in Las Yaguas, where otherwise much the same courting pattern seems to have been followed. In Las Yaguas there were dark pathways, empty houses, even *posadas*,[2] where lovers could meet.

Couples in Buena Ventura would sometimes have sex in the house of one or the other's parents or in the house of a friend. If the parents knew of this, they would certainly not express approval, particularly if nothing had been said about marriage (consensual or legal), but it was not uncommon for them to give tacit consent by "looking the other way" if the couple appeared to have serious intentions about their relationship.

On the whole, then, there was a general acceptance among the people of Buena Ventura of premarital sex. This contrasted with traditional "middle-class" Cuban values, at least insofar as women were concerned, and contemporary government ideology. The revolutionary government strongly supported the sanctity of the marriage bond and the crucial importance of the nuclear family. As for premarital sex, the revolutionary regime dodged the issue as best it could. Fidel Castro told Lee Lockwood: "Traditions and customs can clash somewhat with new social realities, and the problem of sexual relations in youth will require more scientific attention. . . . Neither customs nor traditions can be changed easily, nor can they be dealt with superficially."[3]

Another problem had to do with interracial marriage and the legacy which the postrevolutionary society carried over from traditional Cuban society. If "traditional" Cuban society is taken to mean nineteenth-century Cuba, Martínez-Alier concentrates upon marriage as an indicator of social class and stratification, quoting Edmund Leach's dictum that "in a very fundamental way, we all distinguish those who are of our kind from those who are not of our kind by asking ourselves the question, 'Do we intermarry with them'?"[4] Marriage in nineteenth-century Cuba was, according to Martínez-Alier, ideally isogamic—that is, like married like.[5]

We are, of course, talking about a slave society (slavery was not officially abolished in Cuba until the 1880's) in which the fundamental social distinction was between white and black. Ideally, and according to marriage legislation, nineteenth-century Cuban society was divided into two large groups—those of European origin and those of African descent. Yet in practice, the attribute of color did not classify people clearly into whites and blacks, since there was a high degree of racial mixture.[6]

Official attitudes toward interracial marriage varied. Up to 1864, licenses for marriage between individuals of different racial origins were almost always granted. In 1864 a period of virtual prohibition of interracial marriage began which lasted up to the mid-1870's. Then in 1881 an official decree granted freedom of marriage between the races.[7]

The abolition of slavery and freedom of intermarriage did not, of course, eliminate racial discrimination in Cuba. From late in the nineteenth century to the mid-twentieth century there was by no means a clear-cut hierarchical system of superordination and subordination between the races, but there is no question that, in general, light skin connoted higher prestige than did darker skin. But, as Booth has pointed out, the relevance of physical appearance varied according to the social context.[8]

In any case, in the period after the abolition of slavery in 1880 and during the first half of the twentieth century, marriage and family patterns and race relations have remained a drastically underresearched field. Booth notes that no systematic study of Cuban family and kinship patterns in this century has yet been made. "On the available evidence, however," he claims, "it is clear that in most essentials the pre-revolutionary Cuban family approximated to the norms observed elsewhere in the Hispanic Caribbean."[9]

Nelson elaborated these norms in his 1940's study of (mainly) rural Cuba. He thought the family was particularly important in Cuba because of the weakness or absence of other institutions (for example, the church).[10] For the white elite, family structure was basically patriarchal, with the husband-father the dominant figure over the wife-mother and children. The position of women was defined "in relation to an ideal of submissiveness and constrained by a system of beliefs which wedded the concept of honour to that of virginity."[11] The double standard of sexual morality prevailed, and the cult of masculinity (*machismo*) was widespread.

However, outside the upper strata of society—and particularly within the lower black stratum—there were other forms of domestic arrangements. Common-law unions and extraresidential mating were frequent and, at least in the late nineteenth and first half of the twentieth centuries, morally acceptable alternatives to legal matrimony.[12] Nevertheless, popular attitudes reportedly distinguished sharply between common-law marriages and casual affairs.[13] Common-law marriages were more numerous in rural areas than were legal unions, while in urban regions legal marriages were by far more usual than consensual unions.[14]

In 1968, Verena Martínez-Alier conducted a series of interviews among largely black families in the Sierra Maestra. She found that 95 percent of the couples were living *aplazados,* that is, in free union. Marriage was regarded as the ideal state, but they agreed that "a good *aplazamiento* was better than a bad marriage." Booth encountered a similar attitude in Havana in 1969 among middle-aged blacks.[15]

Of the ninety-four household heads whom we interviewed in Buena Ventura, thirty-nine were living in consensual union, nine were married by civil ceremony, thirty-two were separated or divorced, seven were widowed, and another seven were single, never married. Thus, 41.5 percent of the total were living in consensual union, accounting for 81.3 percent of all married households heads. Legally married couples accounted for just 9.6 percent of the total,[16] while over one-third of the household heads were separated or divorced.

At the time of our census, sixty-seven married couples were living together in Buena Ventura,[17] 13 residents were married to persons living elsewhere, 38 were separated from previous unions, and 17 were widowed. A total of 202 residents of Buena Ventura fifteen years old and over (80.8 percent of those in ninety-four households) reported having been married at some time. Forty-eight men and women fifteen years old and over (19.2 percent), most of them in the fifteen-to-nineteen age group, had not married. Women reported 191 unions and men 151, a total of 342. The mean number of marriages for those who had ever married was 1.7 per person. The range was from 1 to 6 unions per individual. Common-law marriages accounted for 81.7 percent of the total for women and 82.8 percent for men.

Marriage between the races was uncommon in Buena Ventura. Among forty-four household heads, only five were married to partners of different races.[18] In three of these cases, the man was white and the woman nonwhite;[19] in the other two cases the woman was white and the male nonwhite. In twenty-seven cases both the men and the women were nonwhite, and in the remaining twelve the couple was white.

Although we do not have precise figures available now, our census data and genealogies indicated a high incidence of marriage between men and women from within Buena Ventura. Commonly a young man and woman set up housekeeping together before considering a legalized union. This living arrangement was often in the home of one of the spouse's parents. The doubling-up was almost always necessary, at least for a while, since it was almost impossible to get one's own home—even a single room—in Havana. In Las Yaguas the housing situation had been more flexible, since new household members could often add another room to the house. Additions were illegal in Buena Ventura.

When doubling-up became necessary, it was the woman's parents who were chosen more often than the man's. Of twenty-four households which contained a couple or couples living with the parents of one of the mates, twelve lived with the girl's parent or parents and eight with the man's. In three of the households, both a son and a daughter had a spouse living in the home. In one household the couple lived with the bride's foster parents. Excluding single-member households and those containing childless couples, well over half the remaining homes in Buena Ventura contained married children living in the home.

Ideally, a man was supposed to get permission from the girl's parents or guardians before the couple married or began living together, but this ideal was one of many which was seldom realized. If the couple was underage, as aas often the case, and parental approval was not forthcoming, the boy and girl simply began to live together. A young man might consult a girl's parents when the union had become a *fait accompli,* but this would be more a pronouncement than a request.

As is common elsewhere in the Caribbean, men would sometimes wait until the child was born before admitting or denying paternity, looking for the presence (or absence) of some identifying feature which would link the child biologically to the man. In any case, the Constitution of 1940 (and later the Código de Familia) stipulated that children born out of wedlock had the same rights as legitimate children.[20]

Physical violence between spouses, common in Las Yaguas, persisted among families in Buena Ventura. This violence was not surprising among members of the older generation, but its continuance among the younger generation was somewhat unexpected by us, particularly since both men and women had recourse to the People's Courts and there was always the possibility that CDR officials would intervene. Indeed, several women and men had brought their marital conflicts to the local tribunal.

Sexism and *machismo* continued to prevail in Buena Ventura. Men boasted of their sexual conquests, and the double standard persisted. Yet while it is true that the majority of the men, and a good many of the women, expressed the belief that "a woman's place is in the home and a man's place is in the street," there were males of both the younger and older generations who willingly shared household duties and family responsibilities with their spouses. Furthermore, many females of all ages never did adhere to the outlook that women should kowtow to men.

It was mentioned in the beginning of this chapter that thirty-six of the ninety-four households were headed by women; that is, the contract was in their name. This situation was different from that of the "matrifocal" households found in Las Yaguas and discussed in chapter 1. In the old community, because of his weak economic position in terms of earning power, the husband/father often became a marginal member of the household, resulting in matrifocal homes where the woman was the dominant figure. In Buena Ventura, the fact that the house title was in the name of the mother/wife often (but not always) had little to do with authority roles. It could, nonetheless, be a strong bargaining card in disputes.

In summary, nearly one-half the households in Buena Ventura were related through affinal or consanguineal ties; extended-family households were common. This statistic should not, however, be looked upon as evidence of close emotional ties within and between families. The ideal household in Buena Ventura consisted of a husband, a wife, and their children. Extended households and kin ties with neighbors were often the result of the housing shortage in Cuba in 1969–70. Nevertheless, endogamous unions were common within the housing settlement.

Parent-Child and Sibling Relationships

Participant observation and interviews by our staff showed that the mother-child relationship was clearly the strongest tie within the families of Buena Ventura, as it had been within those of Las Yaguas. The precedence it took over the husband-wife bond seems typical of lower-class families (and, perhaps, of most families of any class).[21]

However, unlike the situation in Las Yaguas, where the father was sometimes an inadequate provider and thus may have been a marginal member of the household, in the new housing development he was virtually assured of employment and a steady income. The result was a more stable household.

Both parents, if living together, acted as disciplinarians to their children. Stepchildren created special discipline difficulties, since it was often not clear to parents or children what authority the stepparent could or should exercise over the stepchildren.

Sibling ties were generally weak and mutual obligations vague. There are differences in the literature about the nature of sibling ties in lower-class families. The situation in Buena Ventura—as it had been in Las Yaguas—seemed to have approximated what Rodman found among the poor in Trinidad. Obligations between siblings usually involved little more than a general expectation to help each other in time of need.[22]

For various reasons, responsibilities fell upon children in Buena Ventura at a later age and more lightly than they did in Las Yaguas. The improvement in the economic situation of the families since the Revolution precluded the necessity of children working or begging, and laws against child labor were enforced. There was mandatory school attendance and, though some children in Buena Ventura did not attend, the majority were in classes. Also, since working mothers in Buena Ventura, in contrast to Las Yaguas, were in the minority, housewives were able to perform tasks which in earlier times might have fallen to the children. These tasks were not necessarily only household chores, but income-earning employment and the tending of younger siblings as well. Finally, the conveniences of sanitation facilities, running water, and so forth, meant that fewer hands were necessary to perform essential tasks even though there was a larger living area to care for.

By means of education of the youth and the knowledge by young men and women that they had the promise of secure employment, some of the older authority patterns between parents and children had changed. Youngsters continued to espouse the ideal of obedience to one's parents, yet their actions often belied this belief. For example, in a family with whom the *equipo* had maintained close contact, Jesús Rivera was the butt of jokes by his six children. Although he was only sixty-five years old, his sons and daughters ridiculed him behind his back about being senile and kidded him to his face. They apparently had no intention of being cruel to him and, in fact, usually treated him kindly, but they still mocked him and paid no attention to his orders.

In practice, though not by law, older people tended to be ignored by the Castro regime. As a Cuban informant said to *Chicago Sun-Times* reporter Ted Morgan, "Castro doesn't care about old people because they are not productive."[23] Or, as the title to Marvin Leiner's book reads, *Children are the Revolution*.[24]

Divorce

Even though our data suggest that unions were more stable in Buena Ventura than in Las Yaguas, broken marriages were commonplace in the housing project, and news of separations was rarely greeted with surprise. "Marital shifting" was not infrequent within the housing project. A couple would separate and one of the partners move in with another mate in Buena Ventura, while the other might have someone else move in with him or her. This shifting occurred several times during the course of our investigation, involving both young and older men and women. In one instance, the husband of a fifty-nine-year-old woman left her to live with a woman of sixty-one. In another case, a young man's wife left him and their two children to move in with someone else in the community, with whom she had another child. The deserted partner then invited his neighbor, with whom he had been having an affair anyway, to move in with him. Although she was legally married to someone else—a man serving a prison sentence —she accepted the invitation.

Reasons for separations and divorce were similar to those found in most Western (including Third World) societies: sexual incompatibility, adultery, different role expectations, personality clashes, problems of household management, and so forth. In Havana there was the additional problem of overcrowded housing, which frequently caused friction between husbands and wives, and affinal and even consanguineal relatives. In Buena Ventura itself, the situation was perhaps unusually fluid because it was a generally agreed-upon principle that couples that did not get along together should separate with a minimum of formality.

Relations Between Related Families Within Buena Ventura

It will be recalled that almost half the households in Buena Ventura had some kind of kin in another household in the settlement. Our study of related families living in different households reinforced our impression about the preeminence of the mother-son tie, even into male adulthood. Men were usually highly solicitous of their mothers, making daily visits to their homes, sometimes taking them money, food, or other gifts. This pattern extended beyond Buena Ventura, often linking several of the housing projects through mother-son ties.

Mothers and daughters living in separate homes in the settlement sometimes cooperated closely in socioeconomic affairs. Rosita ("Sita") Franca, for example, cared for the children of her daughter, Celina ("Lina"), while Lina ran errands for her mother or conducted illegal enterprises in her home. This, by the way, was one of the rare instances of daily contact between persons residing on opposite sides of the housing project.

Many of the difficulties already discussed which existed within households also arose between related households. These problems were alternately aggravated and alleviated as family members shifted dwellings. For example, Tomasa Torrente lived with her son Ciro when she met Rubén del Valle, her current husband. Rubén had a daughter, Maida, by a previous marriage who lived with her godmother and godfather, Juana Cruz and Belino Alvarez, near Tomasa's house. Ciro and Maida became *novios* and eventually married. Thus, Rubén was both stepfather and father-in-law to Ciro, and Tomasa was stepmother and mother-in-law to Maida. Ciro and Maida lived in the house of Maida's godparents.

Belino was a blind man of seventy-eight. He and Juana each received a pension of twenty pesos a month, but when Ciro moved in, Belino claimed that the pensions were suspended. So Ciro had to support a household of four on his salary of ninety pesos a month, which he earned as a laborer.

Juana went to work, washing and ironing at other people's homes in Buena Ventura, but this brought in only fifteen or twenty pesos a month. In order to make ends meet, Juana purportedly made forgeries in her ration book to get extra goods to sell. When OFICODA noted the forgeries, Juana, apparently with success, placed the blame on Maida and Ciro. The young couple was sanctioned to be deprived of purchasing clothing for one year.

Shortly thereafter, Maida aborted her first pregnancy and blamed it on the tensions in the house. Later she gave birth to a son. The couple and their infant then moved to Tomasa's house. Tomasa and her son had always been close, and at first she and her daughter-in-law got on well together. However, in sharp contrast to the immaculate household run by Tomasa, Maida proved to be a negligent homekeeper. Tomasa complained to us:

> She'd have things strewn all over their room. Ciro would say to me, "This can't be. This has to stop. You make sacrifices for her and I come home from work tired and find this. No, it can't go on." But it did. Their little kid urinated on the floor, but she wasn't capable of wiping it up right away. She waited until he trod in it and things like that.
>
> She got that from Juana. They're a bunch of pigs. Why she still has a bundle of rotten clothing from Las Yaguas, rotten for twenty years and full of cockroachs and spoiled guavas!

Maida and Ciro decided to move back with Maida's godparents, even though the relationship between the two couples remained strained. They made all purchases separately, cooked apart, and kept separate budgets. The old folks were bitter and blamed the whole situation on Maida for getting married, but they were unable or unwilling to evict the young couple. When Juana left for work, Belino would go to Sita's house to listen to the domino games so he wouldn't have to be around Maida. With Maida out from underfoot, relations improved immeasurably. Maida ran errands for Tomasa, tinted her hair, and cared for her when she was ill. Maida and Ciro were anxious to move to their own home but were unable to find one.

In a number of such cases we reviewed, tensions and arguments brought about by preferences in personal habits and generational differences, exacerbated by rationing and overcrowding, could be (and sometimes were) alleviated or eliminated by shifting living arrangements. The subject of overcrowding is discussed later in this chapter.

Some problems between related households could be traced back to conflicts already existing in Las Yaguas. For example, Marcelo Quintana and his half-brother Camilo had had a very poor relationship for many years. According to Camilo, Marcelo was the one responsible for starting the rumor that Camilo's wife, Blanca, had worked as a prostitute in Las Yaguas to support Camilo. Camilo and Blanca isolated themselves from their neighbors and relatives in Las Yaguas and continued to do so in Buena Ventura. Camilo told his wife not to have anything to do with others in the housing project, claiming there were a lot of problems in the neighborhood that were maliciously blamed on them. Camilo arranged to have their food purchases made in a grocery store ouside the *reparto* so they would not have to be in contact with their neighbors.

Affinal Relationships

The weakest link between related households was the affinal one. Although close friendships were sometimes forged between families through an affinal tie, it was not unusual for these friendships to become strained or broken when the affinal bond dissolved.

Berta Torres and Rufina Rodríguez used to visit each other regularly, commonly exchanging food and cigarettes and helping each other with cooking and other household chores. Rufina's daughter, Ester, was at that time married to Berta's brother Vicente. When Vicente was sent to jail on a charge of possession of marijuana, Ester began seeing other men in Buena Ventura, eventually moving in with Claudio Bromley. Berta took affront at Ester's actions and broke off her relationship with Rufina.

The alternating warmth and coolness of affinal bonds was merely one facet of the vagaries which characterized, but was certainly not peculiar to, interpersonal relations in Buena Ventura. Occasionally we found unmitigated, long-standing hostility between parents and sons- or daughters-in-law. This situation existed mainly between a mother and her son's mate. Leda Moreno and her mother-in-law, Sita Franca, serve as an example.

Leda and Venancio Bustamante, Sita's son, met in Barrio Galiano of the *reparto* Neptuno y Lealtad, where both were living at the time of the Triumph of the Revolution. Although Venancio rented a room there, upstairs from Leda, his official residence was recorded at the home of his mother in Las Yaguas. He maintained his room in Barrio Galiano while working on the construction of Buena Ventura. Even though he had contributed more hours than anyone else in his family to the Buena Ventura project, his mother managed to have the house contract put in her name.

Leda and Venancio entered into a free-union marriage in Galiano, and Leda bore him a daughter. Unfortunately for the couple, Sita made clear her opposition to the union. She had known Leda for a number of years and considered her a libertine. Leda related:

> My problems with Old Sita and her family go back to Las Yaguas. We were always at each other's throats. I was living in the room in Barrio Galiano at the time, but I used to go to Las Yaguas to visit my friends. Every time Sita's family saw me they started a rumpus. They'd say they didn't want any whores hanging around there and that sort of thing. María, the social worker [who worked in Las Yaguas during relocation

of the families] told them that if the trouble continued she'd call the police, but it kept on. Finally I said to Venancio that I didn't want anything more to do with him because of his family. I told him to get out and leave me alone.

"No," he said, „I like you and want you to raise my daughter. Look, I'll go and speak to my mother."

Nothing came of the attempt to smooth things over between Sita and Leda. Leda decided to stay with Venancio and stopped going to Las Yaguas. However, in 1963 Venancio was apprehended by the police for trafficking in marijuana and sentenced to prison.

Leda found herself alone with two children and expecting a third. Despite her problems with Sita, she applied for a housing transfer to Buena Ventura in the expectation that her mother-in-law would care for her children when Leda found employment. The transfer was approved, but Leda's hopes for assistance from her mother-in-law were dashed when Sita declined to oversee the children and refused to recognize Leda as her daughter-in-law.

Leda took a job anyway, leaving her children alone to fend for themselves. Reportedly she locked the children in the house when she left for work and even tied them to the bedstead. Sita finally denounced Leda to the People's Courts, accusing her of abandonment and mistreatment of the children. Leda received a public admonition from the court and was ordered to stop abusing her children.

Toward the end of our investigation, by which time Leda had five children, she summed up her feelings in an interview:

> It's still the same. The other day I went by Sita's house to pick up something Venancio had sent me. As I was leaving, the old gal starts off with, "Your whoring mother." Then she goes on, "You whore, you lesbian, you dike." She grabbed a bucket of water and threw it at me, telling me to clean myself up. I said to her, "The truth is that you're the dirty pig, you're the filthy one, and I'm not coming back here again!" So she said to me, "What I want is to never know anything more of you. And I'm going to break up that marriage of yours by witchcraft or any other means."
>
> I tell you, I don't want anything to do with those people again.

The proximity of the homes of Sita and Leda, the use of the same grocery store and other facilities, and Sita's concern, however ambivalent, for her grandchildren, meant of course, that contact and continued friction between the two women was unavoidable. Leda's main hope was for another housing transfer and public assistance for her children.

It is impossible to conclude from the data how general such a situation was in Buena Ventura. The particular relationship between Sita and Leda could not have been the usual type of interaction between mother-in-law and daughter-in-law, since Sita did not recognize the union. Nonetheless, hostilities between mothers- and daughters-in-law frequently seemed to be the opposite side of the coin of the close bonds between mothers and sons.

Buena Ventura and the Problem of Overcrowding

It should be clear that social relations within and between families often became strained because of overcrowded living conditions and lack of opportunity to choose one's place of residence.[25] This problem was compounded when there were disputes over home ownership. The family of Delfina Puerta is illustrative. Her grandson, Felipe Cueva, had worked a total of 2,179 hours in the construction of Buena Ventura, and for that reason the title to the house was in his name. However, his uncle by marriage, Marcelo Quintana, who also lived there with his wife and son, claimed the house should rightfully be his because he was paying the rent. Felipe put forth his view of the situation this way:

I didn't work on the construction of this *reparto* to have a house so some coxcomb who never did anything could kick me out of my own home. That guy who lives with us [Marcelo] believes that he's the one who has the last word, so he's gone to the Urban Reform to try to get me out.

When Marcelo and I began to live under the same roof, we agreed that he would pay one month's rent, I'd pay the next, and so forth. That's the way we began, but I lost my job and couldn't keep paying. He took advantage of that by paying the rent and complaining that I wasn't paying anything. When I offered to pay for the months that I missed, he said that it wouldn't be necessary.

From that time we began to fight over any little thing. Because of that family my wife has beome unsociable. I wish they [the authorities] would get me a little house around here so I could live alone with my wife. I hardly come by the house at all now except to sleep so I can avoid the problems we have. We have a trial [in the People's Courts] over an accusation I made that Marcelo is using food items that don't belong to him, but he denies that.

Marcelo, who was away on active military duty when Buena Ventura was built, replied:

My room is so small my wife and I have to sleep in the same bed with my boy—a young man of fourteen years. Such a thing is inconceivable, and I'd like to get permission to build a little room onto the back here.

This house has only three bedrooms, and sixty thousand difficulties arise.

For example, the old lady [his mother-in-law] sleeps in one room with her daughter and grandson, and changing clothes is a hassle. The boy takes off his clothes in front of everybody and sleeps nude. He pisses in the corner in the middle of the night if nobody's looking.

My relations in this house are good. The only problems are about things which nobody would like. For instance, there are two radios here, and when I turn mine on at a normal tone, so as not to disturb anyone, those people over there [Felipe and his wife] turn the other one to a different station at a high volume, so this is like a madhouse. Nobody can live like that.

Las Yaguas may have seemed "overcrowded," but there were important differences. First, Las Yaguas was largely "self-built"—that is, within the limits of available resources, people built their homes in the manner they saw fit. Buena Ventura was the product of middle-class planners, designed according to their notions of what type of dwelling was best for relocated slum dwellers.

However, as Hartman noted, physical factors alone have traditionally been stressed by planners in the evaluation of housing conditions and in planning for improved residential areas. Physical factors are important, he added, but they have no invariant or "objective" status and can only be understood in the light of their meaning for people's lives—which in turn is determined by social and cultural values.[26]

A frequently overlooked aspect of this argument is the conception and perception of space. Fried and Gleicher suggest that in the urban middle class, space is characteristically used in a highly selective way:

The boundary between the dwelling unit and the immediate environs is quite sharp and minimally permeable. It is, of course, possible to go into and out of the dwelling unit through channels which are specifically designated for this purpose. But walls are clear-cut barriers between the inside of the dwelling unit and the outer world. And even windows are seldom used for any interchange between the inner world of the dwelling unit and the outside environment (except for sunlight and air). Most of us take this so much for granted that we never question it, let alone take account of it for analytical purposes. It is the value of the "privacy of the home." The dwelling unit may extend into a zone of lawn or garden which we tend and for which we pay taxes. But, apart from this, the space outside the dwelling unit is barely "ours."

As soon as we are in the apartment hallway or on the street, we are on a wholly *public* way, a path to or from someplace rather than on a bounded space defined by a subjective sense of belonging. Beyond this is a highly individualized world, with many common properties but great variability in usage and subjective meaning. Distances are readily transgressed; friends are dispersed in many directions; preferred places are frequently quite idiosyncratic. Thus there are few physical areas which have regular (certainly not daily) widespread common usage and meaning. And contiguity between the dwelling unit and other significant spaces is relatively unimportant. It is primarily the channels and pathways between individualized significant spaces which are important, familiar, and common to many people. This orientation to the use of space is the very antithesis of that localism so widely found in the working class.[27]

The authors add that this common experience and usage may be dominated by a conception of the local area beyond the dwelling unit as an integral part of home. This view of an area as home, and the significance of local people and local places, is so at variance with typical middle-class orientations that it is difficult to appreciate the intensity of its meaning, the basic sense of identity involved in living in a particular area.[28]

The contrast between Las Yaguas and Buena Ventura with respect to the foregoing was striking. Homes in the slum were often of but a single room; however, if living quarters became too uncomfortable, an annex or additional shack was built. But more importantly, the spillover into the patio or street formed the "continuity between the dwelling unit and other significant spaces" mentioned by Fried and Gleicher. This spillover presented to the visitor from outside an appearance of congestion. With some exceptions, however, former residents of Las Yaguas generally failed to report feelings of overcrowding in living and moving space.[29] Las Yaguas resembled the slums of San Juan, Puerto Rico, studied by Oscar Lewis and me, where "living area" included the outdoors almost as much as the indoors.[30]

Buena Ventura was something more than "Las Yaguas built of cement," but, perhaps unconsciously, the phrase captured the feeling of new confinements of space: the louvered windows, the solid walls and doors, the paved streets and concrete pathways. The analogy between the West End of Boston vs. the new housing project there and Las Yaguas vs. Buena Ventura is worth drawing. Herbert Gans called the West End an "urban village,"[31] referring, as Hartman noted, to its "autonomous, self-sufficient qualities, the ability of the neighborhood to provide most of the daily needs (except, in most cases, employment) of its inhabitants. In contrast, the total residential space in a housing project, while larger (courtyards, playgrounds, grass, parking areas, asphalt areas) has the quality of insularity and tightness, precisely because it is all specifically part of the project, all part of one's residence.[32]

Las Yaguas was, like the West End, a community composed of a number of subcommunities. Both Havana's Las Yaguas and Boston's West End could be considered what Suttles called "defended neighborhoods"—residential groups which have sealed themselves off through the efforts of delinquent gangs, by restrictive covenants, by sharp boundaries, or by a forbidding reputation. "Indeed," says Suttles, "it appears that the most persistent characteristic of these defended neighborhoods is their boundaries and the necessity of anyone who lives within these boundaries to assume a common residential identity." Neighborhood identity is a stable judgmental reference against which people are assessed and may necessitate one's explaining one's guilt or virtue by residential association.[33]

Numerous former residents of Las Yaguas related how they lied to friends, lovers, or employers about their place of residence.[34] To come from Las Yaguas was to bear a stigma, a kind of "tribal stigma," to use Goffman's term, which can equally contaminate all members of a family.[35]

Buena Ventura might also be considered a defended neighborhood, but not of the same order as Las Yaguas. Suttles emphasizes that the defended neighborhood is primarily a response to fears of invasion and exists within a structure of mutual opposition to other residential areas. With good reason Las Yaguans feared invasions by police, federal agents, and henchmen of sundry businessmen claiming ownership of the land.[36] In any case, it is the mutual opposition rather than primordial solidarity alone which gives the defended neighborhood its unity and sense of homogeneity.[37]

Buena Venturans lacked the sense of unity which comes from an opposition to outsiders of the type described by Suttles. Indeed, as that author remarked, classical discussions of "community—such as those by Park and his associates (1925), Wirth (1928), Redfield (1955), and other members of the so-called "Chicago school" of sociology and anthropology—left us unprepared for communities, like those created by public housing projects, where the residents may be homogeneous in their social characteristics but lack any strong loyalties to one another."[38] In this respect, the situation in Buena Ventura was somewhat similar to that described by Lee Rainwater for the Pruitt-Egoe housing project in St. Louis. He reported that the residents of the project were ambivalent about their fellow tenants: "They give them credit for trying to make a decent life even as they themselves are doing; yet they have a low opinion of others' ability to accomplish this, or to avoid making trouble even with the best of intentions. This sense of alienation from others in the community was apparent in even the most casual conversations about the project."[39]

Buena Venturans suffered a double alienation: from their neighbors and from the larger society. Las Yaguas was hardly a residential delight, but there was a sense of community and comradeship that was absent in Buena Ventura. As Nicolás Salazar related:

> We here in Buena Ventura are not a community. To build a real community there must be deep understanding and identification between neighbors. There should be sharing and mutual help, like between friends.
>
> We had more community feeling in Las Yaguas; at least my family felt it for those who lived closest to us. People cared when somebody got sick. When one of us was sick, three or four neighbors stopped by every day to ask how we were. When *mamá* was in labor, a neighbor woman came to help deliver the baby. A neighbor always volunteered to take an injured child to the doctor. People were closer and got along better with each other there. There was a spirit you don't find here. I don't know what made the difference. Perhaps because we lived in the same place and were all poor together. Here in Buena Ventura we all live in the same place, but each one feels alone. People act as if they'd gone to a lot of trouble if they so much as say hello. In Las Yaguas nobody interfered with your private life, but here, if they see you fairly often, they want to butt into your life.
>
> The new system of life helped divide families who were on friendly terms with each other because so many neighbors were sent to different *repartos*. I had a lot in common with a family that now lives in Bolívar. In Las Yaguas I'd visit them practically every day and often eat there. But the new *barrios* are so far apart that now sometimes two whole

months pass without my going to see them. So even if our standard of living is higher than it used to be, some of us don't like living in Buena Ventura.[40]

The unpopularity of government-built housing among many of the former slum dwellers of Las Yaguas may be viewed as one more instance of the general lack of success of public housing to solve the problems of adequate shelter of low-income families.[41] This failure may in small or large part be laid to the inability or unwillingness of planners to tailor their principles to the needs of the particular populations they are serving.

As Turner has suggested, the planning concepts derived from the experience of modernized countries are frequently inapplicable under circumstances typical in the modernizing nations. Among other things, the principle of "minimum modern standards" is based on the assumptions that high structural and equipment standards take precedence over high space standards and that the function of the house is, above all, to provide a hygienic and comfortable shelter.[42]

Also, many of the low-income families, who are usually part of a relocation scheme, are multiproblem families with needs extending far beyond the exigencies of shelter. Fried and Gleicher observd: "The belief that poverty, delinquency, prostitution, and alcoholism magically inhere in the buildings of slums and will die with the demolition of the slums has a curious persistence but can hardly provide adequate justification for the vast enterprise of renewal planning."[43]

Many Buena Venturans held a nostalgic attachment to Las Yaguas. This seems to be a common reaction of people relocated from slums to new hoising projects. In his study of former inhabitants of Boston's West End, Fried states that for the majority it was quite precise to speak of their reactions to the loss of their old neighborhood as expressions of grief, "the sense of helplessness, the occasional expressions of both direct and displaced anger, and tendencies to idealize the lost place.[44]

Oscar Lewis' touching portrait of a young Puerto Rican mother who moved from a San Juan slum to a new government housing project illustrates the difficult problems of adjustment in her new environment and helps us understand why, in spite of the efforts of well-meaning governments and the spending of huge sums of money on public housing, the positive effects hoped for by social planners are not always forthcoming.[45]

Notes

1. *Compadrazgo,* or godparent relationship, was weakly developed among families in Buena Ventura.
2. Inns where rooms could be rented by the hour.
3. Lee Lockwood, *Castro's Cuba; Cuba's Fidel,* p. 106. Upon taking office, Prime Minister Castro initiated a campaign to legalize all common-law marriages. The Ministry of Justice formed committees to wed, sometimes in mass ceremonies, couples living in consensual union. The number of legal marriages increased dramatically in the years following the Revolution, as did the number of divorces, as divorce laws were liberalized.
4. Verena Martínez-Alier, *Marriage, Class and Colour in Nineteenth-Century Cuba,* p. 119.
5. *Ibid.,* p. 19.
6. *Ibid.,* p. 71.
7. *Ibid.,* pp. 31–40.
8. David Booth, "Neighbourhood Committees and Popular Courts in the Social Transformation of Cuba" (Ph.D. diss., University of Surrey, 1973), p. 288.
9. *Ibid.,* pp. 220–21. This contention is controversial. Still moot is the question of the extent to which one may generalize marital and family relationships, as well as race relations, throughout the Hispanic Caribbean. For example, Gordon K. Lewis observed that "traditionally the Puerto Rican family, at all levels, has been a variant of the older forms of European familial organization, relatively unaffected (*as compared with the family in other Caribbean societies*) by native Indian or African Negro customs" (Gordon K. Lewis, *Puerto Rico: Freedom and Power in the Caribbean,* p. 264; my italics). Other viewpoints and considerations may be found in works by Ames, González, O. Lewis, MacGaffey and Barnett, Nelson, M. G. Smith, and R. T. Smith listed in the bibliography.
10. Lowry Nelson, *Rural Cuba,* pp. 174–75.
11. Booth, "Neighbourhood Committees," p. 221.
12. *Ibid.*
13. Wyatt MacGaffey and Clifford R. Barnett, *Cuba: Its People, Its Society, Its Culture,* p. 63.
14. *Ibid.,* pp. 63–65. See also Foreign Policy Association, *Problems of the New Cuba.*
15. This survey by Martínez-Alier was cited by Booth, "Neighbourhood Committees," p. 223. Booth's finding is on the same page.
16. Civil marriage is the only legally recognized marriage in Cuba.
17. For purposes of this study, marriage is considered to be a union between a man and woman engaging in sexual intercourse, generally with the recognition of the community, with an assumption on some permanency in the relationship. Usually, economic cooperation exists between the partners, and paternity of any offspring resulting from the union is acknowledged by the genitor (cf. George Peter Murdock, *Social Structure* [New York: The Free Press, 1949], pp. 1–8). "Marriage" and union are here used coterminously except where it is necessary to distinguish between legal marriage and free (consensual, common-law) union—a usage followed by our informants.
18. The race of one member of four couples heading households was undetermined.
19. Nonwhite includes both mulatto and Negro.
20. Certain exceptions in the 1940 Constitution were eliminated in the Código.
21. As Helen Icken Safa noted for a San Juan slum, "Given the strong segregation of conjugal roles and the weakness of the marital relationship, the emphasis is not on

the emotional tie between husband and wife, but on the intensity of the mother-child relationship, which persists long after the children are grown and have families of their own" (*The Urban Poor of Puerto Rico: A Study in Development and Inequality*, pp. 47–48).

22. Hyman Rodman, *Lower-Class Families: The Culture of Poverty in Negro Trinidad*, pp. 94, 98.

23. Ted Morgan, "Cubans' Love Story with Castro Continues," *Chicago Sun-Times*, Dec. 16, 1974, p. 2.

24. Marvin Leiner with Robert Ubell, *Children Are the Revolution: Day Care in Cuba.*

25. This is not to suggest that overcrowding is always a source of friction or that strained relations are always caused by crowded living conditions.

26. Chester Hartman, "Social Values and Housing Orientations," *Journal of Social Issues* 19, no. 2 (1963), 130.

27. Marc Fried and Peggy Gleicher, "Some Sources of Residential Satisfaction in an Urban Slum," *American Institute of Planners* 27, no. 4 (1961):311–12.

28. *Ibid.,* p. 315.

29. This is similar to Hartman's findings in the West End of Boston: "Paradoxically, then, housing project residential space, while objectively more open and less densely populated than the West End, was viewed as congested and overcrowded, because of the lack of meaningful structuring, the abrupt differentiations, and the apparent absence of controllable diversity with regard to personal and spatial elements" (Hartman, "Social Values," p. 285).

30. I have described how housing vocabulary plays a prominent part in English loanwords adopted by former slum dwellers of Puerto Rico living in New York. Loanwords such as *hall, closet, window, landlord, tenant, basement, ground floor*, etc., reflect the fact that housing was one of the most significant differences between the new environment in New York and the Puerto Rican homeland (Douglas Butterworth, "English Loanwords in Puerto Rican Spanish," unpublished manuscript).

31. Herbert J. Gans, *The Urban Villagers: Group and Class in the Life of Italian-Americans.*

32. Chester Hartman, "The Limitations of Public Housing," *American Institute of Planners Journal* 29, (1963):285.

33. Gerald D. Suttles, *The Social Construct of Communities*, pp. 27–36.

34. See, for example, the life histories of Alfredo Barrera and Nicolás Salazar in Oscar Lewis, Ruth M. Lewis, and Susan M. Rigdon, *Four Men: Living the Revolution: An Oral History of Contemporary Cuba.*

35. Erving Goffman, *Stigma: Notes on the Management of Spoiled Identity*, p. 4.

36. See the story of Lázaro Benedí in Lewis, Lewis, and Rigdon, *Four Men*, for an example of police invasions of Las Yaguas.

37. Suttles, *Social Construct of Communities*, p. 58.

38. *Ibid.,* p. 12.

39. Lee Rainwater, *Behind Ghetto Walls: Black Families in a Federal Slum,* p. 100. Susan Rigdon pointed out to me that the situation is not exactly comparable since these tenants had not known each other for many years while living together in another community.

40. Lewis, Lewis, and Rigdon, *Four Men*, p. 445.

41. There are, of course, exceptions to this statement. For an eclectic overview of public housing around the world, see Charles Abrams, *Man's Struggle for Shelter in an Urbanizing World*. For Europe and America, see J. S. Fuerst, ed., *Public Housing in Europe and America*. For the U.S.S.R., see Alfred John Dimaio, Jr., *Soviet Urban Housing: Problems and Policies*. There is no adequate summary for Latin America,

although Abrams is useful. For Puerto Rico, see Chester Hartman, *Family Turnover in Public Housing,* and for Cuba, the works of Jean-Pierre Garnier, *Une ville, une révolution: La Havane, de l'urbain au politique,* and Maruja Acosta and Jorge E. Hardoy, *Urban Reform in Revolutionary Cuba,* are of some utility.

The term *public housing* is technically incorrect when applied to the Cuban situation described here. By *public housing* is usually meant housing owned by the government, which leases the dwellings to the public, generally at an expensive rate. In Buena Ventura and other related projects, the people were buying their homes and apartments. Nevertheless, for purposes of this discussion, Cuban government-built housing may be considered a kind of public housing.

42. John C. Turner, "Barriers and Channels for Housing Development in Modernizing Countries," *Journal of the American Institute of Planners* 33 (1967):167.

43. Fried and Gleicher, "Some Sources of Residential Satisfaction," pp. 305–306.

44. Marc Fried, "Grieving for a Lost Home," *The Urban Condition: People and Policy in the Metropolis,* ed. Leonard J. Duhl, p. 151.

45. Oscar Lewis, "Even the Saints Cry," *Trans-Action* 4, no. 1 (1966):8–23.

5

Community Relations

Friends and Nonfriends

Nonkinship networks in Buena Ventura were characterized by regular face-to-face encounters and tended to reach "closure." That is, starting with person A and tracing his or her personal network through B, C, and D, D would eventually articulate with A.[1]

To illustrate, Sita Franca exchanged almost daily visits with her neighbor, Matilde Betancourt. Matilde also associated frequently with Jimena Alford, who, in turn, was a friend of Elvira Alvarado, the last a steady visitor to Alejandra Díaz' home. Alejandra often saw Celina Cesas, Sita's daughter. Although they lived on opposite sides of Buena Ventura, Celina saw her mother every day.

Women's networks were activated for the usual socioeconomic purposes: borrowing food items or small amounts of cash; using a stove, electric iron, or some other appliance; chatting over a cup of coffee; listening to the radio. There were also the important rationed food item exchanges and visits for purposes of gambling, drinking, and spiritual consultations.

Men's networks were somewhat more loosely knit than women's, principally because most adult males worked outside the settlement, and some formed friendships with fellow workers. But for most men, the majority of their friends lived in Buena Ventura or in one of the other six *barrios* of resettled Las Yaguans. There was, in fact, a tremendously complex network linking men—and women—in the seven housing projects. But aside from traditional family ties and friends from Las Yaguas, there was the added consideration that many of the men did not feel accepted by their fellow workers because of their former affiliation with Las Yaguas.

Most visiting in Buena Ventura took place within one's own block. The most intensive social interaction took place in the block between República Street and Bondojito, particularly the middle of that block, where Alejandra Díaz lived. Alejandra's house was the most popular in Buena Ventura because of Alejandra's charm, hospitality, and knowledge of *santería*. Her home was also said to be a gambling center. It was not unusual to find six or seven visitors at her place whenever one of our staff dropped by. Alejandra's house was humorously referred to as the New Social Circle. In contrast, the western part of the block had little social intercourse. This was where the single elderly men were concentrated.

Although there were genuinely warm, long-lasting friendships within Buena Ventura, there was also a generalized feeling of suspicion and hostility towards many of one's neighbors. Conflict between neighbors was a repetitive theme expounded upon by our informants. There were complaints about arrogation of communal plots, stealing of fruits and vegetables from gardens, theft of animals, misuse of community facilities, and so forth. A typical complaint was voiced by Alfonso Cruz:

> Next door there's a fellow named Alfredo Barrera. There's been a whole series of problems existing between us. He's always spreading rumors. One time the drain in my patio was clogged up and I was trying to fix it, even though I know very little about that kind of thing. But I had no choice, since I didn't know anyone who could help me.
>
> Well, I ended up making things worse because when I started digging with my pick to uncover the drain, I hit a water main, opening up a hole in it. The water began to spurt out, and I was alarmed for a moment, but I grabbed a handful of mud and stopped it up. I told Barrera what had happened.
>
> Barrera had the same problem with his drain that I had, and a few days later several of the houses behind mine were flooded. My neighbors started fighting with one another, each putting the blame on the other.
>
> Then the lady in front of Barrera, Fermina, said that it was his fault because he had opened a hole to get his drain unclogged. He said that wasn't right, that I had put a hole in the main right here in my own patio, so I was the one to blame. Later I learned that Barrera had been the one who had created the whole problem by clogging up his own drain, but the word had already been spread about me by that woman's mouth.

That's why I distrust my neighbors. They never treat you the same. One day it's one way, the next day another, and you never know what the reason is. Take my next-door neighbor, Matilde. She's a little bit like this fellow Barrera. I used to be friends with her, like I was with Barrera, and his family were great friends with Matilde's. But something happened around Christmas, I don't know what because I was away, but they had an argument—Barrera and Matilde—and stopped seeing each other. I was still on good terms with Barrera.

Since I wasn't interested in what had happened, I continued to treat everyone the same when I came back. But there was a kind of jealously there, that if I continued treating Matilde as before, or Barrera as before, one or the other would stop speaking to me—and that's exactly what happened. We became distant. They both stopped speaking to me and I to them.

And I want to keep it that way, too, because I'm the kind of person who carries a grudge. If I'm friends with somebody and he does something that doesn't sit well with me, I remember that forever. Even though I might make up with him, I'm not going to treat him like I did before. So to avoid that and to have a less hypocritical relationship, I simply wish that those people would never speak to me again.

Clearly, arguments such as these could take place almost anywhere. But there were a couple of things which made the altercations in Cuban housing projects such as Buena Ventura somewhat different. Misunderstandings between neighbors were probably as common in Las Yaguas as in Buena Ventura, but in the former, arguments were usually settled by the individuals themselves or through intervention of friends and kinsmen. But in the new housing projects (and elsewhere) there was always the possibility of being denounced to one of the CDRs and maybe brought before the People's Courts.

Furthermore, the knowledge that a government repair agency might take weeks or even months to get around to looking into a problem of maintenance or replacement of parts (if it did at all) meant that people were highly sensitive to property damage, whether intentional or not. As for intent, causing damage to property or wasting resources was no light matter in Cuba in the 1960's and 1970's.

Even though distrust ran deeply, and hostilities erupted with some frequency among the residents of the housing settlement, the consensus was that there were only a handful of families in Buena Ventura that were constantly in the center of the disorders and who were considered to be incorrigible troublemakers.

Sulema Ferrer's family had the reputation of being among the worst offenders in this respect. Sulema's house was a continual focus of "scandalous behavior," as neighbors were wont to say. The language and demeanor of the fifty-six-year-old woman and her daughters in public places, such as the grocery store and bakery, where their middle-class neighbors "from above" also shopped, were cause for dismay among many residents of Buena Ventura.

CDR President Abelardo Fuentes reported that Sulema had been charged with starting a fight in the local bakery. Three times she was ordered to appear before the People's Court; three times she failed to comply, yet they did nothing to her. "You sure can't deny she's from Las Yaguas," commented Abelardo. Sulema herself admitted: "I'm always fighting. When it's not for one thing it's for another. The truth is I fight because I want things done my way. I'm just not myself without a fight on my hands. When I'm quiet and calm, people ask me if I'm ill. "You're sick, Sulema. What is it?" "Nothing," I say. "I just don't feel like a fight. I don't feel like shouting. That's my personality."

Yet there was another side to Sulema which contradicted her bad reputation. Observation by our field workers strongly tended to support the opinion held by some of her neighbors that, to be sure, Sulema was cantankerous and outspoken, but she was not normally a troublemaker. She was actually a hard-working, self-sacrificing woman. Sulema took in washing and ironing to support her family, which, besides Iria and Paloma, the two daughters living in the house, included one of her sons, Mario, and four grandchildren, offspring of Iria and Paloma. In addition to caring for these members of the household, Sulema helped look after two former husbands who lived in Buena Ventura. One of them, Dario, was seventy-one years old and lived alone. Sulema took meals to his house daily and cleaned up after him. The other, Fernando Santillana, lived with one of their daughters, Felicia. They frequently ate at Sulema's house. While Sulema was occupied with these tasks, Iria and Paloma walked around the housing project in ill-fitting miniskirts and baggy sweaters, flirting with men in Buena Ventura and workers in the adjacent construction depot, perhaps inviting them to their home.

Sulema frequently became exasperated at the behavior of Iria and Paloma. She and her daughters would hurl verbal brickbats at each other and, on more than one occasion, we witnessed Iria and Paloma physically attack their mother. Sulema would either cry or retaliate aggressively. In either case, they would eventually make up and, characteristic of families in the housing project, usually unite in the face of adversity.

For example, at one time during our study Paloma was living with a young man, Nemesio Casas. Toward the end of the investigation, Nemesio broke off with Paloma and took in another woman, Teresa Portes. However, Nemesio and Paloma saw each other occasionally to have sexual relations. At the same time, Paloma was sleeping with other men in the *reparto*. When the twenty-year-old girl became pregnant with her third child, she announced that Nemesio was the father. Nemesio (and most other people we talked to) thought this was merely a ruse on Paloma's part to get her man back, or at least have him acknowledge paternity and support the child.

When he refused, Paloma and her sisters, her brother, and her mother marched on Nemesio's house to force a showdown. A fight ensued between members of the two households, during the course of which Paloma was stripped of her clothing and a rock, apparently aimed at Teresa, struck Nemesio's mother, gashing her forehead. The battle ended only when the police arrived.

Iria and Paloma seemed to fit perfectly the stereotype held by outsiders of the kind of young women who lived in Buena Ventura, and, even though residents of the settlement shook their heads in mock disbelief at the girls' behavior, most of them allowed that such were the ways of people with a Las Yaguas heritage.

Some of the younger men and women of Buena Ventura made no pretext of their disdain for the pettiness and backbiting of their fellow residents. These youngsters, in their late teens and early twenties, dressed nicely, dated partners from outside the community, and openly criticized their neighbors to others. As a result, they were roundly disliked by most of the populace of Buena Ventura. As twenty-one-year-old Ester Salinas told us: "They hate me in Buena Ventura. Practically everyone who lives here can't bear the sight of me because I don't associate with anybody here. My friends are from outside the *reparto*. I dress well and make myself up attractively and I'm never without a pretty dress or a new pair of shoes. Believe me, I've exchanged a few hot words with the people here. Some of the girls have tried to scratch my eyes out and I've tried to do the same to them. But outside of my *reparto* everybody treats me well."

Another woman who did not conform to the expected behavior of Buena Venturans was seventeen-year-old Lala Betancourt. She had numerous boyfriends from different parts of Havana. She went to "high-class" places such as the Tropicana night club, frequently arrived home late, or not at all, and never invited her friends into the *reparto*. She was a favorite target of gossip in the neighborhood.

In order to understand better the people of Buena Ventura, an important point to observe here is that they viewed the actions of Lala and the daughters of Sulema in an entirely different light. It was acknowledged that Iria and Paloma were libertines, but this was somehow all right because they conducted their affairs in Buena Ventura, mainly with residents of the settlement. Everyone knew who came and went with the girls. But Lala was a pariah because she went out with men from elsewhere and, unlike most other women in the settlement, refused to discuss her personal life with her friends or neighbors. In short, she had departed from the norms of Buena Ventura, and people were not willing to forgive her for that. There were perhaps feelings of envy, inferiority, and rejection on the part of Lala's neighbors.

Young women were not the only "nonconformists" in Buena Ventura. Ejidio Salinas, Ester's younger brother, had a woman friend in Havana and another in Camagüey with whom he stayed whenever the opportunity arose. He avoided close contacts with both men and women in Buena Ventura. "Friends?" he replied to one of our inquiries. "I don't have any here. I have a ton of acquaintances, but no friends. I know my neighbors, but I never visit them. I don't go to anybody's house here except my sister's."

There were also adults who held themselves aloof from their neighbors. Most of these were not from Las Yaguas and had moved to Buena Ventura through *permutas* (housing exchanges). There were several, however, who were raised in the former slum but nevertheless felt no affinity for their fellow Buena Venturans. Socorro Granados, a thirty-four-year-old woman, was one of these. The only person that Socorro visited, and the only friend she had in Buena Ventura, was her next-door neighbor, Lourdes, a relative newcomer to the housing project. The two helped each other in various ways, visiting daily back and forth. Otherwise, Socorro did not trust or confide in anyone in the settlement.[2] She felt rejected by other people in Buena Ventura, and she, in turn, rejected them, particularly her half-sister, Alejandra

Díaz—perhaps because Alejandra was so popular with her neighbors while Socorro was not.

A symbolic manifestation of Socorro's attitudes toward her fellow residents was found in the clothing she made. She was a seamstress who sewed for people both within and without the settlement, mainly the latter. We observed that the clothes Socorro made for outsiders were of high quality, imaginative, and attractive. But what she made for people in Buena Ventura were, in the words of one of our student assistants, *"porquerías"* and *"chambonas"*—a patchwork of poorly made garments. Socorro, incidentally, sewed for Alejandra and Alejandra's sister-in-law, Marisol Casas, and charged them "up to the last centavo" for shabby goods.

Socorro herself dressed better than her neighbors (who were ridiculed by "those from above" for their outmoded attire), as did her two children, whom she did not allow to associate with other children in the neighborhood.

In Socorro's boyfriend we could see another aspect of her isolation from others in Buena Ventura. Her friend was from outside the settlement and dressed "as if he were from another time and place." His dandyish attire included a well-pressed white suit, starched shirt, wide-brimmed hat, highly polished shoes, and gold watchchain with a huge medallion attached to it. With his long fingernails and gold teeth, he, as one of our staff observed "looked just like a pimp out of Batista's time." He would pick up Socorro in a taxi and bring her home the same way. Neighbors were at once bemused and resentful of her actions, especially since she had been brought up among them in Las Yaguas.

Gossip and Sex

From what has been said, it should be apparent that there was a permissive attitude toward sex in Buena Ventura, but, as in any community, this attitude was hedged with restrictions. Sexual liaisons within the housing project, if not accepted by all inhabitants, were at least not usually condemned if they did not involve close relatives (immediate affines and blood kinsmen up to and including first cousins), were not with members of the same sex, and were not adulterous (the last particularly applicable to women and especially within Buena Ventura). Behavior along any of these lines—referred to by the residents as an *escándalo* (scandal) if they learned about it—was usually accompanied by gossip, that universal mechanism that conveys both morsels of information and expressions of disapproval.

Max Gluckman discerned that "it has taken the development of anthropological interest in the growth and break-up of small groups to put gossip and scandal into their proper perspective, as among the most important societal and cultural phenomena we are called upon to analyze."[3]

The recording of community gossip has a long tradition in anthropology. Elsie Clews Parsons published nearly one hundred pages of town gossip she heard in Mitla, Oaxaca, during her three visits from 1929 to 1933. "From these impressions," she wrote, "will be imparted, I hope, some appreciation of the disposition of the townspeople, what they laugh at, what they are willing to talk about, and what they keep to themselves; what interests or gratifies them; the kind of behavior they condemn, the kind they commend or are indifferent about; how they feel about customs they know are lapsing; their manners and conventionalities."[4]

Among the more popular items of gossip in Buena Ventura during our stay were that CDR President Abelardo Fuentes was the lover of his mother-in-law; that Panchita Saenz was entertaining young men in her home while her husband was out; that Ramón Fajardo had fathered a child by the mentally retarded daughter of Delfina Puerta; and that Ramón's daughter-in-law had been having sexual relations with her stepfather. There were also accusations that, among others, Avelardo Alvarez and Miguel Fonseca were homosexuals and Rufina Rodríguez and Alejandra Díaz were lesbians.

The list could be expanded, but it is sufficient as it stands to point up some of the sexual mores of residents of the housing project: affinals ·and step-relatives were included in the incest taboo; wives were not to have extramarital affairs (husbands could, but with discretion); men should confine their sexual advances to women who could "defend themselves" (*defenderse*); and homosexuality was to be censured or ridiculed. As for the last, there was a strong revulsion toward homosexuals, common throughout Cuba and, it would seem, wherever *machismo* is found. Martin Loney observed, "The Cuban—indeed the Latin American—attitude to homosexuality is extremely simple: it is regarded as a form of human degradation."[5]

Lesbianism was held in about the same disrepute as homosexuality in men. Leda Moreno expressed what seemed to be the general attitude on the subject in Buena Ventura:

> One day a neighbor told me that she had heard my stepdaughter Silvia telling her friend Lourdes that she had been in a house where she saw a man with an erection. Lourdes said to her, "Ay, girl, don't you know that doing it with girls is so much better than with men?" Silvia asked what it was like, and her friend said that it was just heavenly.
>
> Later I talked to Silvia and asked her what was wrong with her. I told her that I would never think of discussing things like that and that any woman with such a lack of values and judgment deserves to die. I realized that I had to treat her like a woman, not the little girl she is, so I was harsh with her.
>
> Lourdes really upsets me. Even a prostitute caught in the act can't be criticized as much as a lesbian. A whore is a thousand times better than a dike, and that's what I told my stepdaugher. I said that even though I've been with a lot of men, nobody could accuse me of being a lesbian, and that I'd rather be known as a whore than a dike.

At this juncture I should like to look at one event which occurred in Buena Ventura during our stay to see what it might indicate about attitudes of the residents toward one another. According to what was told us (we did not witness it), nineteen-year-old Darina Rivera was enticed to smoke a marijuana cigarette by some male visitors to the housing project. After smoking the marijuana, Darina went to her house with one of the men. She had a goddaughter, Marta, staying with her, but her husband, Lorenzo, was away cutting sugarcane and her father-in-law, Jesús Rivera, was also absent. So, aside from Marta, the house was empty.

Apparently Darina went to bed with the man, but then Marta started to cry. Darina's brother-in-law, who lived nearby, came over to the house, thinking the child was ill. When Darina didn't answer his calls, he looked in the window and saw her having sexual relations with a man. At first he thought the man was her husband, but he lit a match and discovered it was someone else. As he lit the match, Darina shouted, "Don't light matches, I'm having too much fun!"

In the hubbub that followed, Darina's lover escaped from the scene as people from the neighborhood quickly gathered, lighting matches, while Darina shouted, "Don't light matches! Turn out the light!"

Several of the spectators went to fetch Darina's father and brother. They led her, wrapped only in a towel, to Jesús' home. Next morning they sent for Darina's husband. When Lorenzo arrived, his father told him what had happened, but Lorenzo didn't believe it. He said that Darina would never do such a thing in her right mind, that the drug must have been responsible.

A few days afterward, Darina went to the grocery store with her sister. People from Buena Ventura began taunting her, crying, "Put out the matches! I'm having fun!" The "people from above" who patronized the same store could, of course, only conjecture what was behind the taunts. This taunting happened every time a member of Darina's family went to the grocery, until one day her sister said to the baiters, "Well, her husband was cutting cane, and Fidel said that no stalk should be left standing. So my sister decided she should do her part by harvesting stalks here in Havana."

There are a few things to note about this entire event. Darina was one of the nonconformists of Buena Ventura, and her neighbors jumped at the opportunity to verify their worst suspicions about Darina. Smoking marijuana (if this was true) may have been reprehensible, but to make matters worse, she had not only committed adultery, but had done so with an outsider. Had the act been perpetrated by, say, one of Sulema's daughters (while living in a marital state), there would have been little notice taken, and most likely the matter would never have been alluded to outside the confines of Buena Ventura, surely not for a period of several weeks. In essence, what the inhabitants of Buena Ventura were saying was, "You see, she's no better than we are, after all."

Crime

Robbery was the crime most often cited in Buena Ventura. Neighbors were those almost invariably suspected of the offenses, and these suspicions were probably correct, since outsiders were easily spotted in the housing project. Petty thefts of fruits and vegetables from a family's garden plot were constant sources of irritation among the populace. The stealing of chickens or other fowl was more serious, but less common. CDR President Abelardo Fuentes told us that 150 pesos' worth of chickens had been recently stolen from him. Sabino Cruz and his wife had a television set stolen while we were there. They were not from Las Yaguas, disliked their neighbors intensely, and managed to get transferred out of the housing project after the burglary.[6]

Fights between families in Buena Ventura were commonplace, and police intervened when things got too rowdy. It was not unusual for a belligerent resident to be taken to police headquarters for questioning and, occasionally, arrest. Our observations and interviews with informants indicate that the police were restrained, even indulgent, toward the population of the housing project. In any case, most altercations between neighbors were settled out of court, often through intervention by CDR officials, even if minor bodily injury had been sustained.

There were, however, some serious crimes committed by residents of Buena Ventura both inside and outside the housing project. One of Ester Salinas' mates, for example, went to prison for stabbing a boy in Havana. Cuco Casas was arrested on various occasions for theft and breaking and entering. The eighteen-year-old youth did not work and was considered to be among the worst juvenile delinquents in the settlement. Several cases of violent assault within the housing project were pending in the People's Courts.

Sulema's sons had notorious reputations. Jesús Rivera talked about them:

> They'll take anything. When we were building this place, one of the men in charge of cutting wood noticed that his eyeglasses had disappeared. We had to stop everything and search the place. They were found because everyone knew Mario [Sulema's son] had been hanging around there and that he was a thief. And just last week the police picked him up again at his house. He had committed a robbery near Batabanó. He broke into a warehouse, cut open the sacks with a knife, and took all the food.
>
> And that brother of his! He and Mario went up to a house on Baragua Street where the people had chickens, turkeys, and a pig out back. Mario and Pablito cut the fence with pliers and left the man with nothing. And there was a guy ui here "above" who sold bread and fritters. Mario robbed him of three hundred pesos, but Dávalos and Darina's husband saw him four days later and took the money away from him.[7]
>
> Those boys don't work. They live by stealing. Now they're going to go to work in agriculture for a while so they can get their labor census cards. But after a while they'll stop working again.
>
> Nobody can raise animals, because those types jump over the fence and carry them off. You can't have anything here. I have some areca

palms that I've been cultivating for a long time because I enjoy growing things. There's a lady who comes here to buy them and sometimes she brings other people who want an areca palm for decoration. That helps out a little with my small salary,[8] but I don't go out to sell them. That's not allowed now. But if I weren't careful, somebody would take them.

I can't even raise roses here because people come and cut them. I had my wife put out a red cloth by each rosebush, and when one of those types came along I said, "Look, *compañero*, those roses are dedicated to Santa Barbara." He went away and never came back. That trick worked pretty well.

Gambling, Drugs, and Drinking

Gambling in any form was forbidden by the Castro regime, but there were at least six homes in Buena Ventura which served as gambling centers, all run by women. Sita, her daughter Celina, and Jacinta Blanco ran lotteries in their houses. Other women held card and dice games in their homes. A new and popular game at the time of our study was based upon the sugarcane harvest. The volume of cane harvested each day was published in the daily newspaper *Granma*, and bets were placed on the last two or three digits of the figure. The homes of Rufina Rodríguez and Alejandra Díaz were centers for this activity. Many residents of Buena Ventura were against the illegal gambling but voiced their objections only infrequently to their neighbors because of a desire not to cause problems and because of fear of reprisals.

Most of the homes hosting gambling activities were also centers of other illegal pastimes. Sita and her daughter, for example, reportedly sold marijuana and bootleg liquor, and Celina operated a black market. Her husband had been convicted for possession of marijuana and sent to a rehabilitation center. Jacinta Blanco's husband had been imprisoned for trafficking in drugs. Juan Tomás' house was reputedly both a gambling house and a marijuana distribution center.

Most of the buyers came from outside Buena Ventura. Although marijuana was readily available in the settlement (reportedly some was grown in a field adjacent to the *reparto*), drug abuse could not be considered a serious problem among the people of Buena Ventura. Similarly, heavy drinking was uncommon in the housing project. Alcoholic beverages were expensive and difficult to acquire legally, although, as mentioned earlier, bootleg rum was manufactured in Buena Ventura.

Santería and Curing

As in Las Yaguas, residents of Buena Ventura practiced Catholicism, spiritism, and *santería*. Most Buena Venturans considered themselves Catholics, though they did not attend services.

The Roman Catholic Church (the Vatican as well as the church in Cuba) originally supported the Revolution, but the "honeymoon" lasted less than a year. When the Vatican and Cuban prelates expressed concern about the increasing suppression of religious freedom on the island, Castro rejoined that Catholic churches were undertaking criminal campaigns against the Revolution. He denounced priests as Fascists and Falangists and told the church to stick to philosophy and religion and leave politics to him.[9]

It was reported that in the Bay of Pigs invasion of April 17, 1961, two Catholic priests accompanied the invaders as chaplains. In the next couple of days, several prelates and dozens of priests were arrested by the revolutionary government, and churches were temporarily closed. Six weeks later the government nationalized private education and confiscated church and Catholic school property. Castro prohibited religious processions and announced that any priest involved in politics would be deported. The following months saw the exodus of hundreds of priests and nuns from Cuba.[10]

Though the Catholic Church was the main target of the Communist attack, Protestant groups also came under fire. As Nelson remarked, "undoubtedly the most indigestible group for the revolution has been Jehovah's Witnesses. . . . The Witnesses very early came under the condemnation of the regime for refusing to salute the flag. . . . According to *Newsweek* magazine, this refusal stimulated Castro to exclaim, 'We cannot tolerate this irreverence to the Fatherland.' He further accused the sect of being an agent of the CIA."[11]

The confrontation between church and state lasted for several years. However, beginning about 1965, and continuing through the period of our study, tensions were reduced, and a period of coexistence ensued. Churches were permitted to reopen, and services were held regularly. But proselytizing was outlawed, and the youth of Cuba was indoctrinated with atheistic dogma. A number of our younger informants in Buena Ventura declared themselves atheists. There was no Evangelical movement in the housing project.

Since the Revolution, public recognition has been given by the government to Afro-Cuban religions as an element of the national cultural heritage.[12] *Santería*, the syncretism of African and Roman Catholic deities, was (apparently) widely believed in by the people of Buena Ventura. We can only conjecture how widespread this belief was because of the secrecy involved in performance of its rituals—a secrecy partly traditional and partly the result of disapproval by the government. (The apparent contradiction between the public recognition given by the revolutionary government and the fear of disapproval on the part of the people is only one of the paradoxes of the Revolution. In this case, the paradox was that between the doctrine of scientific rational thought as one path toward the creation of the "New Cuban Man" and respect for Cuban folk beliefs and practices.)

Anyway, we know that at least one-quarter of the households had *santería* paraphernalia; however, it does not follow that all members of these homes were active or avid practitioners. Further, there were households without *santería* symbols whose members visited other homes in the settlement to witness or participate in the rituals. People from other *repartos* visited some of the more renowned centers of *santería* in Buena Ventura, and residents of the housing project, in turn, visited homes in other parts of Havana. (Spiritism in Cuba was of minor importance, particularly as compared to that in other Caribbean countries such as Puerto Rico.)

Slaves introduced from Africa into the New World brought with them many of their customs and beliefs, including religious practices. In most countries, native African religious beliefs, at least in their outer manifestations, were stamped out; however, in a few nations such as Brazil and Cuba, African religious practices survived with surprising vigor.

As practiced in Cuba, the gods in *santería* are called *santos*, in Spanish, and the men and women who work with them are *santeros* and *santeras*. The equivalents in Yoruba are *orisha*, *babalorisha*, and *iyalorisha*.[13] The African elements of *santería* are predominantly Yoruba, or Lucumi, as the Yoruba of Nigeria are called in Cuba.[14] The European traits are derived mainly from Roman Catholicism. The African slaves attempted to conceal pagan religious practices behind a Christian façade. The initiation rituals, divination techniques, chants, and myths are non-Christian, but the Christian calendar is used for religious rites, and devotees of *santería* are baptized before initiation into the cult.[15] Thus emerged a syncretism of African and European religious traditions.

There are also "Congolese" and other influences in Cuba, such as vodun (voodoo) of Dahomeyan origin (modified in Haiti), but the Yoruba element has remained dominant.[16] Bastide comments that "of all the African religions which have persisted in America, without doubt it is the religion of the Yoruba which has remained most faithful to the aboriginal model."[17] In New World *santería*, the Christian God became assimilated into the Yoruba sky god Olofin, and the offspring of Olofin became identified with the Holy Trinity. In each case, the identification of *orishas* with saints was accompanied by a complex, not always consistent, interweaving of the corresponding mythologies and rituals.[18]

Stones are of fundamental importance in Cuban *santería*. Bascom notes that while chromolithographs and plaster images of the saints are prominently displayed on shrines in the homes of the *santeros*, they are regarded as only decorations. The real power of the saints resides in the stones, without which no *santería* shrine could exist. The stones of the saints are believed to have life, and some stones can walk, grow, and even have children.

The saints are fed with food, blood, and herbs. Each saint has its own particular herbs, own type of stone, and favorite food animals. Blood is the food of the saints. The stones are the objects through which the saints are fed and in which their power resides. There are certain saints who are fed through objects other than stones—for example Ogún, for whom iron is used.[19] Cigars and other forms and products of tobacco are placed as offerings for the saints, and water and alcoholic beverages are offered to quench their thirst.

The spirits of dead relatives are important objects of attention and worship in the practice of *santería*. Each worshiper has his or her own patron saint, chosen by divination or to suit his personality or because his family regards a particular saint as its ancestor and guardian.

The ritual in *santería* ceremonies varies according to the inclination of the *santero*, "from an imitation of Catholic ritual, complete with candles, the Lord's Prayer, Hail Mary, and appropriate ritual gestures, to the deliberate creation of a hysterical atmosphere in which the *santero* and other persons present are 'possessed' by the spirits." In initiation rites, blood sacrifices of animals take place.[20]

Santería's appeal has been mostly to the black population of Cuba, although it has a following among whites, particularly those in the poorer sector. Afro-Cuban religious ceremonies were widespread in predominantly black Las Yaguas.[21]

Santería in Buena Ventura

With the advent of rationing and later the abolition of private businesses after the Revolution, it became increasingly difficult to make the necessary offerings and sacrifices to the *orishas*. This was a severe blow to the professional standing of *santeros* and to those aspiring to initiation rites. However, devotees often went to painstaking and time-consuming lengths to acquire the desired materials for a ceremony. Francisca Muñiz from Buena Ventura tells of her efforts to arrange a fiesta in honor of her saint:

I organized the party for the twenty-third of the month because it was the birthday of my *santo*: I had completed two full years of being with Yemayá. The first year's birthday I couldn't do anything because it was so difficult for me to go get everything. I had to acquire it little by little. I began to save money last year to buy the animals and the food, the rice and the beans. My niece Eveliss' husband helped me. He went to the country to get six pounds of beans for me. A girl who visits here brought me two pounds of rice. Mamá gave me some bottles of oil. Rosa's husband gave me three coconuts, and my godfather gave me four candles. My sister Alma gave me cocoa butter and the white dress which I wore. I bought everything else.

I had to buy the chickens, the guinea hens, the sheep, the goats, and the doves. I had to work hard to get those animals. I'd order them from anybody who might know where to get them. I told them if a goat was for sale to let me know.

I don't really know how much money I invested because everything was bought in bits and pieces. I bought the little goat from Fajardo and it cost me fifty pesos. The large goat, the one for Ochún, I exchanged for the she-goat I used to have. That exchange was made with the *güajiro* who lives out back here. I'm still in debt for the sheep. Another gentleman who lives here brought me half a dozen doves which cost me fifty pesos. The guinea hen also cost fifty pesos. In addition I had to sacrifice cocks and hens, but they were mine. There were four hens and five roosters. I borrowed the stew pots, the plates, the table settings, and everything for the throne setup—the handkerchiefs, the tablecloths, the bedspreads, everything.

There's a symbolism of colors used in the throne. Blue is for Yemayá, white for Obatalá, and red for Changó. At the rear of the throne is a bedspread which is for any saint because it has all the colors. The one in front is for Ochún because it's yellow.

In my religion, the only things which are like the statues [of the Roman Catholic Church] are the Eleguá. There are other stones, and each one has a name. We don't have images or statues or pictures like the Church has. Things are symbolically represented by the colors and in the stones, but not by things which could have been made by man. I don't know why it's that way.

The practice of *santería* serves a number of functions. Clearly it satisfies an inner need of a religious nature among the people. It has also an obvious and very important social meaning to the residents of Buena Ventura and elsewhere. Social networks are created and maintained because of *santería*, both within and without the settlement. Also, practitioners, especially those who become *santeros*, are accorded high prestige among those who believe in or respect those religious practices.

The future of *santería* in Buena Ventura, and in Cuba generally, will depend partly upon government policy, whether it be one of tolerance or suppression of Afro-Cuban beliefs and practices, and, in connection with this, the degree to which continuity takes place in these practices between the older and younger generations.

Disease and Curing

As part of its religious appeal, *santería* had certain healing or curative practices involving biopsychological phenomena such as trances and use of medicinal plants. Herbs constituted a central part of *santería* and curing in Buena Ventura. As Bascom mentioned, "a knowledge of the properties and uses of the herbs is as important to a *santero* as a knowledge of the rituals, the songs, or the language."[22] An *orisha* may be called upon directly, or, more usually, through a medium, to diagnose an illness and prescribe an herb for the cure. The herb would generally be taken internally, but it could be used externally as well. One of the most influential *santeras* in Buena Ventura was Sita Franca. Sita's special gift was her ability to exorcize spirits that possessed people, causing them to fall into a trance. Accompanied by a mystic communion with the *orishas*, Sita would stroke the victim with a branch of the paradise plant (Justicia velutina), thereby extracting the spirits.

It was common in Buena Ventura, with or without the advice of a *santero*, to try home remedies first to cure a malady, and then, if those proved to be unsuccessful, to go to a medical doctor. Herbs usually had first preference, since they often could be prepared in a few minutes, sparing the afflicted person the time and trouble of a medical diagnosis and long waiting periods at the clinic. Adaís Iriarte, for example went to a *santero* in Buena Ventura during our study because one of her sons was sick. The *santero* said that the boy had "an incarnate being" in him, and prescribed a certain herb. The herbal prescription, however, did not cure the boy, so Adaís took him to a medical doctor. The boy was diagnosed as anemic and treated successfully. Adaís professed that she would no longer consult a *santero* for diagnosis of illness.

In Buena Ventura there were many home remedies which had little or nothing to do with *santería*. Table 10 lists the ones we were able to identify, with their uses.

Table 10. Identifiable Medicinal Herbs Found in Buena Ventura and Ailments for Which They Are Used

Herb	Ailment
Artemisia (*Artemisia*)	upset stomach
Rosemary (*Rosemarinus*)	liver ailments
Canna (*Canna warscewiscz*)	upset stomach
Purging cassia (*Cassia fistula*)	common cold
Sickle senna (*Cassia tora*)	gas
Day flower (*Commelina elegans*)	sugar in the blood and kidney ailments
Globe amaranth (*Gomphrena globosa*)	head cold
Barbados nut (*Jatropha curcas*)	inflammations
Bellyache nut (*Jatropha gossypifolia*)	kidney ailments
Justicia (*Justicia*)	nerves
Tick clover (*Desmodium: Meibomia barbate*)	tenesmus
Purple sweet basil (*Ocimum basilicum*)	sugar in the blood
Holy basil (*Ocimum sanctum*)	stomach pains
Sweet marjoram (*Majorama hortensis*)	upset stomach
Pedilanthus (slipperflower) (*Pedilanthus tithymaloides*)	sore throat
Guava (*Psidium guajava*)	throat irritations
Fringed rue (*Ruta chalapensis*)	upset stomach
Garden sage (*Salvia officinalis*)	headaches
Agati sesbania (*Sesbania grandiflora*)	common cold
Black nightshade (*Solanum nigrum*)	ulcers and pimples
Sterculia (*Sterculia*)	chest colds
Verbena (*Verbena*)	liver ailments

Herbs were commonly used to help induce abortions in unwanted pregnancies. Although under certain conditions abortions were legal in Cuba, and generally free of charge, women in Buena Ventura still tended to turn first to home remedies. For example, thirty-two-year-old Leda Moreno had attempted at least six abortions between 1960 and 1968, aborting successfully on four or more occasions. She took potions of beer and grapefruit in an unsuccessful attempt to avoid giving birth to her first son. A year later she gave birth to a daughter, despite her attempts to miscarry.

Of Leda's successful abortions, the first two were induced by a mixture of herbs and juices. That was so painful that Leda thought she might not pull through: "I thought I was going to die. I began hemorrhaging and made a brew of *saldiguera*, sugarcane syrup, and honey, boiled it, and took it for consecutive mornings. It tasted awful and I had terrible cramps. After a week it (the fetus) "dropped." I took the neck of my uterus and expelled it." Leda performed her other self-induced abortions by injecting a solution of water and vinegar into her uterus with a pump. She unsuccessfully tried to abort her last two children.

Notes

1. See Elizabeth Bott, *Family and Social Network*, for a discussion of this aspect of networks.
2. When Socorro was first interviewed, she claimed that she had no relatives in Buena Ventura. It turned out that she was Alejandra Díaz' half-sister.
3. Max Gluckman, "Gossip and Scandal," *Current Anthropology* 4, no. 3 (1963): 307.
4. Elsie Clews Parsons, *Mitla, Town of Souls*, p. 387.
5. Martin Loney, "Social Control in Cuba," in *Politics and Deviance*, ed. Ian Taylor and Laurie Taylor, p. 55. According to a member of our *equipo*, when he was a student at the Pedagogical Institute in the early 1960's there was a purge of homosexuals. He said that about seventy students suspected of being homosexuals were expelled.
6. According to the Cuban government, the incidence of crime, particularly crimes of violence, had been markedly reduced since the Revolution. There are no reliable statistics available to back up this contention (prerevolutionary figures on crime rates are unreliable, and the postrevolutionary press avoids reporting crime), but observations generally confirm that murder, rape, and assault had greatly diminished. Crimes against property were, however, a problem. Thefts were doubtless related to the scarcity of consumer goods. Juvenile delinquency was a focus of government concern, and Fidel Castro devoted major parts of some of his speeches to delinquency.
7. Dávalos and Darina's husband were both officials in the CDR.
8. Jesús earned niney pesos a month as a street cleaner.
9. Lowry Nelson, *Cuba: Measure of a Revolution*, p. 157.
10. Carmelo Mesa-Lago, ed., *Revolutionary Change in Cuba*, p. 404.
11. Nelson, *Cuba*, pp. 158-59.
12. David Booth, "Neighbourhood Committees and Popular Courts in the Social Transformation of Cuba" (Ph.D. diss., University of Surrey, 1973), pp. 256–57.
13. William R. Bascom, "The Sociological Role of the Yoruba Cult Group," *American Anthropological Association Memoir* no. 63 (1944): 64.
14. Many Yoruba were taken to the New World very late in the slave trade, which apparently is one of the reasons why the worship of Yoruba deities persists in recognizable form in some of the Americas. William R. Bascom, *Shangó in the New World*, p. 5.

15. Booth "Neighbourhood Committees and Popular Courts," p. 242.

16. *Ibid.*, pp. 242–44.

17. Roger Bastide, *Las Américas negras: Las civilizaciones africanas en el Nuevo Mundo*, p. 112.

18. Booth, "Neighborhood Committees and Popular Courts," p. 244. In Cuba there are at least two variations of *santería*: the Regla Ocha and Regla Conga. The Regla Ocha is more purely Yoruban in its derivation, while the Regla Conga is derived partly from the Bantu. There is, in addition, a secular Afro-Cuban organization, the Abakuá. The Abakuá is an all-male secret society, apparently unique to Cuba but perhaps modeled on secret societies of eastern Nigeria. Bastide has shown how African traits survived and became modified in various degrees in different parts of the New World (*Las Américas negras*, pp. 13–47). Further, there is some disagreement among both scholars and practitioners of the religion concerning attributes, identification between Christian saints and Yoruba deities, and gender. Some *orisha* are "bisexual" and many Catholic male saints are shown wearing "female" robes (Wyatt MacGaffey and Clifford R. Barnett, *Cuba: Its People, Its Society, Its Culture*, p. 247).

19. William R. Bascom, "The Focus of Cuban santería," *Southwestern Journal of Anthropology* 6, no. 1: 67.

20. MacGaffey and Barnett, *Cuba*, pp. 249–50. Booth elaborates: "The central figure in the day-to-day religious practice of devotees of *santería* is the lowliest grade of 'priest' or 'priestess,' the *babalorisha* or *iyalorisha*—or, colloquially, *santero* or *santera*. The principal function of this person—in Cuba today it is most often a woman—is to supervise the ritual by means of which new devotees are initiated into the cult. Popularly known as *hacerse el santo*, the process whereby the novice is 'presented' to a selected *orisha* and becomes his spiritual descendant, lasts for several days and entails months of preparation during which the *iyawó* [candidate for initiation] is required to shave his or her head and wear all-white garments. The 'presentation' itself calls for a painstaking ritual purification of *iyawó* and a *toque de santo*, a fiesta with drummers in attendance, in the course of which he or she is expected to be 'possessed' or 'mounted' by the *orisha*. . . . A good deal of food is consumed at such gatherings, and a good deal more is required to be 'offered' to the *orisha* on pain of displeasing him" (Booth, "Neighbourhood Committees and Popular Courts," pp. 263–64).

21. See the story of Lázaro Benedí in Oscar Lewis, Ruth M. Lewis, and Susan M. Rigdon, *Four Men: Living the Revolution: An Oral History of Contemporary Cuba*, for an account of a *santero* in Las Yaguas.

22. Bascom, "The Focus of Cuban Santería," p. 66.

Part III

COMMUNITY INVOLVEMENT IN REVOLUTIONARY
ORGANIZATIONS AND PROGRAMS

6

Education

Primary and Secondary Education in Buena Ventura

At the time of our survey, sixty-three of eighty-four children from Buena Ventura, six to fourteen years of age, were attending school. Five children in this age group (6.0 percent) had never been enrolled in school, while sixteen (19.0 percent) were not going to classes. Thus, about one-fourth of the children under fifteen years of age had either dropped out or had never entered school.[1] This figure may, however, be a little misleading, for a few of these "dropouts" were children temporarily not attending classes (perhaps for months or even years) for family reasons while others stayed home because of a classroom and teacher shortage. Leda Moreno's nine-year-old daughter, for example, was not attending school because her mother wanted her to watch the house while she was at work. Drop-outs and stay-at-homes often said they intended to return to school some day. In any event, the dropout, nonattendance, never-enrolled rate was significantly high in this age category.

Only nine of forty youngsters in the *reparto* (22.5 percent) from fifteen to nineteen years of age were attending school, three of them at night. Six of these held government secondary school scholarships; another held a vocational scholarship.

Of the 239 people fifteen years old and over living in Buena Ventura on whom we have reliable data about education, just 70 (29.3 percent) had completed or gone beyond primary school (sixth grade), and only 10 (4.0 percent) had finished basic secondary school (ninth grade).[2] Of the last group, 6 had gone on to professional or technical training. The highest technical level attained was by Alfonso Cruz, who was in his first year of electrical engineering under the Worker-Farmer Educational Program.[3] The highest professional degree was obtained by Caridad Fuentes, who completed the teacher training program.

Tables 11, 12, and 13 show the educational levels attained by different age groups of residents of Buena Ventura. Clearly, the trend is for higher achievement among the younger people. For example, 30 percent of the fifteen-to-nineteen age cohort had gone beyond the primary level (and nine were still attending school); about 15 percent of the age group twenty to twenty-four had completed more than six years; and 7 percent of those twenty-five years and older had gone beyond primary school. The illiteracy rate shows a similar decline as one proceeds from the older to the younger generations.

Reasons given by both parents and older children for nonattendance in school were often vague and defensive. The most usual excuse for dropping out of school was that education was not worth the bother (*"no vale la pena"*) once literacy had been achieved (there were only three illiterates in the age group ten to nineteen). Teenage dropouts (usually with the consent or active insistence of their parents) often considered it more desirable to work than to continue in school. Youths who began their studies at a relatively older age frequently dropped out of school as they reached their middle teens.

Although the majority of families in Buena Ventura thought their children received adequate instruction and attention from the teachers, a number of parents were quite bitter about the treatment their sons and daughters received. A mother complained that one of her sons was expelled from school for disciplinary reasons. She requested that he be punished but not expelled and asked that the director sign a statement giving his reasons for the expulsion. The result was, she stated, that the director backed down and readmitted the boy.

Another woman complained of racism. She said that black children were not treated like white children. Her black fourteen-year-old daughter was suspended from school for two weeks because she fought with a white student on two occasions. "In this case," the woman remarked, "the director could have resorted to another punishment without taking the student out of classes."

Some of the problems faced by parents and children in Buena Ventura were similar to those found throughout Cuba. There was a severe teacher shortage as a result of the increase in students and the exodus from the island of a large number of teachers in the years after the Revolution. Many of the teachers were inadequately trained, were

Table 11. Educational Level in Buena Ventura Age Group Fifteen to Nineteen

Years Completed	Male	Percentage	Female	Percentage	Total	Percentage
0	0	0.0	1	5.3	1	2.5
1–3	1	4.8	3	15.8	4	10.0
4–6	12	57.1	11	57.9	23	57.5
7–9	7	33.3	2	10.5	9	22.5
10 or more	1	4.8	2	10.5	3	7.5
Totals	21	100.0	19	100.0	40	100.0
Not known	2	—	0	—	2	—

Table 12. Educational Level in Buena Ventura Age Group Twenty to Twenty-four

Years Completed	Male	Percentage	Female	Percentage	Total	Percentage
0 (illiterate)	0	0.0	1	6.3	1	3.7
0 (literate*)	1	9.1	0	0.0	1	3.7
1–3	2	18.2	5	31.3	7	25.9
4–6	8	72.7	6	37.5	14	51.9
7–9	0	0.0	3	18.8	3	11.1
10 or more	0	0.0	1	6.3	1	3.7
Totals	11	100.0	16	100.0[†]	27	100.0
Not known	2	—	1	—	3	—

*Alphabetized during the Literacy Campaign.
[†]Rounded.

Table 13. Educational Level in Buena Ventura Age Group Twenty-five and Over

Years Completed	Male	Percentage	Female	Percentage	Total	Percentage
0 (illiterate)	6	6.6	8	9.9	14	8.1
0 (literate*)	4	4.4	1	1.2	5	2.9
1–3	27	29.7	35	43.2	62	36.0
4–6	44	48.4	35	43.2	79	45.9
7–9	8	8.8	2	2.5	10	5.8
10 or more	2	2.2	0	0.0	2	1.2
Totals	91	100.0[†]	81	100.0	172	100.0[†]
Not known	4	—	2	—	6	—

*Alphabetized during the Literacy Campaign.
[†]Rounded.

overworked, and thus lacked time to improve their skills. The Cuban government admitted that lack of discipline, including cheating, laziness, and lack of attendance, was a major problem. In 1969–70 it was estimated that there were four hundred thousand youngsters between the ages of six and sixteen not attending school, including two hundred thousand between the ages of twelve and fifteen.[4] This situation tended to detract somewhat from the tremendous achievements in education by the revolutionary government.

The Literacy Campaign

In September, 1960, the first Declaration of Havana declared the right of every child to a free education, and later that month, in an address before the General Assembly of the United Nations, Premier Castro outlined plans for adult education. At the same time, he announced that 1961 would be the "Year of Education" aimed at launching an all-out offensive against illiteracy.

The Cuban government realized that to wipe out illiteracy, which stood at close to 25 percent, in a single year was a formidable, almost awesome task.[5] Most observers agree that the success of the program was one of the most spectacular of all reforms—educational or otherwise—carried out by the Castro government.[6]

The primary burden for carrying out the literacy campaign fell on the shoulders of some 125,000 *alfabetizaeores* and 100,000 *brigadistas*. The *alfabetizadores* were mostly adults who volunteered to teach (often in their spare time) in the cities and towns. The *brigadistas* were primarily young volunteers who were recruited from school and trained quickly to serve as teachers for the duration of the campaign. They lived and taught in rural areas.

The *alfabetizadores* and *brigadistas* were augmented by some fifteen thousand "Patria o Muerte" worker *brigadistas*,[7] urban workers who served as teachers in more remote areas while their fellow workers filled in for them on the job. Finally, some thirty-five thousand schoolteacher *brigadistas* were enlisted to provide technical and administrative guidance and serve in organizational positions.[8]

At the start of the campaign, there were 979,207 illiterates in Cuba. By the end of the year, over 700,000 had been taught to read and write. In a single year the illiteracy rate had been lowered to 3.9 percent.[9] Armando Hart, former Cuban Minister of Education, boasted, "Cuba is the first nation of Latin America that can proclaim, with well-earned pride, that it is a country with practically no illiteracy."[10]

The Literacy Campaign in Las Yaguas

Urban slums such as Las Yaguas received high priority in the Year of Education. *Alfabetizadores* went into Las Yaguas armed with enthusiasm and propaganda, explaining the advantages of literacy and painting slogans such as *"Viva Cuba! Sin Analfabetos"'*—"Long live Cuba! Without illiterates."

García Alonso claimed that the literacy brigades had, on the whole, little success in Las Yaguas. She wrote that she met only one woman in her 1963 survey who continued to practice what she had learned during the Year of Education. Others who had been taught the rudiments of reading and writing had forgotten what they knew just two years earlier.[11]

Our data from Buena Ventura reflect a somewhat brighter picture than that painted by García Alonso. Six informants—five men and a woman—had retained the reading and writing skills they had learned some eight years earlier during the Literacy Campaign. On the other hand, sixteen adults over fifteen years of age—seven men and nine women—had reverted to illiteracy or, in some cases, had refused to cooperate with the campaign.

In 1969–70, school children from Buena Ventura still had to put up with the reputation that they or their parents were from Las Yaguas. The primary school was located adjacent to the middle-class *"reparto above"* and students who were not from the housing project (the majority) deprecated the pupils from Buena Ventura. The usual term referring to them was "those from the Las Yaguas block."

The director of the school was aware of the problems and implied that most of the blame lay with the youngsters from "the Las Yaguas block." He maintained that tests had been run on the three hundred students matriculated in the primary school and that seventy-nine of the pupils tested—all from Buena Ventura—were diagnosed as mentally retarded or suffering from severe psychological disturbances. We were unable to verify this claim, but if it is true, it surely bespeaks of a testing situation something less than bias-free.

There were problems with lack of teachers and absenteeism among both pupils and teachers. The director reported that student attendance on any given day never exceeded 85 percent of enrollees and was often considerably lower. He said that he had difficulty maintaining sufficient teaching staff. At the time of our study, the school offered classes from kindergarten through the fifth grade. There was no one available to teach the sixth grade. Because of commuting problems, teachers frequently missed classes.

The director of the school, in an interview with our staff, stated that the children from Buena Ventura used foul language, fought, lost their books, failed to study, and skipped classes. Furthermore, he complained, it had been up to him to teach them basic hygiene practices. He said that the Parents' Council (Consejo de Padres) often visited the homes of pupils who did not attend school and spoke to the parents and absentee students, but little was accomplished because so few of the household heads in Buena Ventura ("perhaps 3 or 4 percent") were "exemplary parents."[12] The CDRs were supposed to help with school attendance, but they neglected this duty along with others (see the following chapters).

Children who attended secondary school were also subjected to occasional discrimination because of their origins. Paula Marcos, a fifteen-year-old girl in her first year of secondary school, told us: "There are a lot of *compañeros* in the school I go to who mention Las Yaguas, and frankly it hurts me. They say this, that, and the other thing about the place and tell me not to hang around with kids from there, so I feel absolutely ashamed to be from that environment. But what can I say, when I was born and bred there?"

Scholarship Students

During the 1960's and early 1970's an increasing number of youths in Cuba were receiving government scholarships. In 1970 there were some three hundred thousand of these scholarship students (*becados*). Those with full scholarships received room, board, clothing, medical care, and a monthly allowance. They lived in boarding houses (often homes in Havana of formerly rich families who had left Cuba), attended classes daily, had to maintain a high academic average, and were subject to strict disciplinary rules.

At the time of our study, ten youngsters in Buena Ventura were *becados*: six boys and four girls, ranging in age from ten to eighteen. Seven of the scholarship students were in boarding schools in Havana, two brothers were in a work-study scholarship program on the Isle of Youth,[13] and a seventeen-year-old had a vocational scholarship.

Not everyone who wanted or needed a scholarship received one. Limitations on funds, administrative red tape, and a continuing *personalismo* were among factors which, combined with criteria such as previous academic performance by the children and integration of the parents in revolutionary organizations, could mitigate against even the neediest applicants obtaining scholarship assistance.

Leda Moreno, for instance, was the thirty-two-year-old mother of five children (discussed in chapter 4) employed in a Havana hospital. Her husband, it will be recalled, was serving a prison term for trafficking in marijuana. Although Leda was a member of the block CDR where she lived, she was inactive in the organization and reportedly was one of the least revolutionary people in Buena Ventura. Her children were regarded as thieves by other families in the *reparto*. One of the interesting aspects of Leda's case was the inherent contradiction between the real need for day and/or night care for her children and the virtual certainty that she would not receive such aid because of her reputation and that of her children. She spoke of her dilemma:

> I've given up hope of getting scholarships for my children. I've done everything I can think of, talked to the authorities, written letters, and everything. I just don't know where else I can go. At first I thought my work center would help me solve my problem, but they didn't help at all. So I decided to look for another way out. I went to see the social worker, but she sent me to her superior, saying that only she could resolve my problem. And that was really a crime because I just got left in the lurch. So from there I went to the police, and they sent me to another lady—I don't know who she was—who told me she could give me only semiboarding scholarships.[14] But I told her my children needed full scholarships since I work on shifts. It really seems unfair that I spend my days taking care of other people's sick children while my own wander in the streets. I'm not putting down the Revolution, just stating the facts.

Adult Education

When the Literacy Campaign ended, a program was instigated to elevate the educational level of workers and farmers. Primary and secondary schooling was offered on farms, in factories, in offices, and in night schools. Courses in self-improvement (*superación*) were made available to more than one-half million adults to bring them up to a third-grade educational level. Adults who finished the third grade were encouraged to join the Worker-Farmer Educational Program in which they could complete the sixth grade. Those who graduated from the sixth grade could continue in the program through secondary school and later continue into vocational school or the university.[15]

This ambitious undertaking meant still another crash teacher training program. Young people or adults with an intermediate education were recruited and trained through a program of two "seminars." The first, the Intern Training Seminar, lasted two to three months and was devoted to an intensive general preparation. The other, called the Permanent Seminar, was held every week.[16]

Alfonso Cruz took part in the program. He had been an unmotivated student who had dropped out of school when he was eleven years old to help support his family. He had completed just three years of primary education. Alfonso married at the age of eighteen to escape problems at home—a drunken father and a nagging mother. The Revolution triumphed shortly after his marriage. He told us:

> My life before the Revolution was nothing more than my work and my home. I didn't read newspapers or have any idea of the political or economic situation, which didn't interest me anyway. I did hear that there had been some kind of rebellion in Oriente and that somebody called Fidel Castro had taken up arms, but it was a superficial kind of thing and I never thought much about it.
>
> My friends were just like me. All they worried about was their own lives. It must have been due to the low level of education of people like us from Las Yaguas that we didn't have a clear idea of things. We didn't know anything about the developments that could occur, the transformations that a society can undergo. We just thought our world would stay the same forever.
>
> I never had any desire to continue my education until after the Revolution. There was a guy at work named Marco Placeros. He too was married and had two or three children at that time, and we began to work together. He was very intelligent and liked studying, and he encouraged me to move in that direction. He even started giving me classes right there in the factory. He began to teach me division, decimals, fractions, and all that. He encouraged me to register in a night school, and that's what I did.
>
> I enrolled in the third grade in a school near Figueroa. Later on they started the Worker-Farmer Education Program in the factory, and I

got through the sixth grade there. I also enrolled at night in a nuns' school—I think it was called the Immaculate Conception—on the Calzada de Balaquer, over in Luyano.

After that I enrolled from 8:00 to 10:30 at night in a Worker-Farmer Secondary School until I passed the course.

But when I tried to enroll in the Worker-Farmer College at the Vedado Institute, I failed the examination and I was a little discouraged. I didn't have any place to go from there because I had already passed the course in the Achievement and Secondary School programs, and the only thing left was to enroll in the college. So I quit studying, although I still have the idea of preparing myself a little more to see if I can pass the exam.

Shortly after this interview was made, Alfonso passed the exam and entered his first year of electrical engineering, a pre-university program.

As with most other Revolutionary programs introduced into Buena Ventura, the attempt to popularize adult education met with only limited success. Long work hours and demands for voluntary labor, not unique to Buena Ventura, probably detracted from incentives to attend night school; however, in the housing project long hours and extra work were also convenient excuses, for some, not to participate in the program.

Notes

1. Age is a factor here, since some parents wait until their children are well past six before enrolling them in school.

2. The Cuban national system in effect at the time of our study was as follows. There were two preschool grades and national primary schools, grades one through six. After primary school, two educational streams diverged. The general stream included basic secondary schools (grades seven through nine), preuniversity institutes (grades ten through twelve), and finally, the university level (a varying number of years). The professional stream included schools for primary teachers' training (three- to five-year programs), technical-industrial schools, agricultural-veterinary institutes, language institutes, centers of physical education and sport, institutes of administration and commerce, and technical-industrial institutes. See Richard Jolly, "Education," in *Cuba: The Economic and Social Revolution,* ed. Dudley Sears; and "Cuba, El Movimiento Educativo 1967–68," *Informe a la XXXI Conferencia Internacional de Instrucción pública convocada por la OIE y la UNESCO.*

3. See the section on adult education.

4. Nelson P. Valdés, "The Radical Transformation of Cuban Education," in *Cuba in Revolution,* ed. Rolando E. Bonachea and Nelson P. Valdés, pp. 445–46; *Granma,* January 20, 1969, p. 2; August 23, 1970, p. 5.

5. According to the Cuban census of 1953, one-quarter of the population ten years old or older had never attended school and less than one-fourth had completed primary school. The remainder—just over half the population—had dropped out of primary

school sometime during their first six years. While it is true that the illiteracy rate had decreased slowly over the first half of the twentieth century, from about 44 percent at the turn of the century to 23.6 percent in 1953, the absolute number of illiterates had increased, from about 690,000 in 1899 to over one million in 1953. The census of 1953 showed illiteracs in rural areas to be almost twice the national average.

Valdés observed that literacy figures do not provide an accurate picture of the state of Cuban education before the Revolution. He believes that a more useful index of education development is the percentage of the population which is enrolled in primary, secondary, and higher education. In proportion to its total population, Cuba had more primary students enrolled in 1923 than it did thirty years later. By 1958 approximately 49 percent of the Cuban children of primary school age (six to fourteen years) had no education (the average for Latin America was 36 percent). Only 24.2 percent of the total population fifteen years old and over ever went to school. Thus, almost three-fourths of the Cubans were either illiterate or had failed to complete primary school. Valdés, "Radical Transformation," pp. 423–24.

6. Excellent analyses of the literacy campaign are contained in Jolly, "Education," and Richard R. Fagen, *The Transformation of Political Culture in Cuba.*

7. Patria o muerte ("Fatherland or death") is a national sloan of Cuba.

8. Fagen, *Transformation of Political Culture,* pp. 10–11.

9. In some cases, literacy meant little more than the ability to write one's name.

10. Armando Hart, "Educational Progress in New Cuba," *Political Affairs* 42, no. 5 (1963): 39.

11. Aida Garci4p´a Alonso, *Manuela la Mexicana,* pp. 10–11.

12. An "exemplary parent" was one who insured that his/her children attended school regularly, dressed appropriately, cared for their books, and so forth, and who maintained an active interest in the school, including concern about children of other families who were lax in attendance.

13. The Isle of Youth, better known as the Isle of Pines, had been the focus of an experiment by the Union of Young Communists to develop a model socialist community. The island had its own budget and staff. The union recruited and supervised all the island's manpower: workers, teachers, and students. Howard I. Blutstein, *Area Handbook for Cuba,* p. 101.

14. In semiboarding schools the students return to their homes in the evenings.

15. Hart, "Educational Progress," p. 39; Valdés, "Radical Transformation of Cuban Education," p. 429.

16. Movimiento Educativo, *Informe,* p. 77.

7

Committees for the Defense of the Revolution

Following the triumph of the Revolution, revolutionary organizations for the masses were established throughout Cuba; among them were Popular Defense, the Federation of Cuban Women, and Committees for the Defense of the Revolution. At first there was skepticism toward these organizations in Las Yaguas, but then some enthusiasm was generated at the idea of a new society based upon participation of the masses.

By the spring of 1963, Las Yaguas no longer existed; its populace had been relocated in the seven new housing settlements in Havana. Despite the fact that the Committees for the Defense of the Revolution (CDRs) and other organizations had been established in Las Yaguas several years earlier, it became clear that few of the relocated individuals had any idea of the purpose of these organizations. The government took great interest in the relocation experiment and, at least in the beginning, went to considerable lengths to imbue the people with revolutionary ideology.

The government assisted Buena Ventura by sending representatives to speak to them, encouraging adults to attend night school, showing films and giving small parties in the Community Center of Buena Ventura, and sending social workers to the housing project to inquire into their needs. In all, the people of Buena Ventura seemed to be flattered by these attentions, and many responded by cooperating with the officials. Residents of the housing development helped

This chapter is based on my article, "Grass-Roots Political Organization in Cuba: A Case of the Committees for the Defense of the Revolution," appearing as chapter 8 in *Latin American Urban Research: Anthropological Perspectives on Latin American Urbanization*, ed. W. A. Cornelius and F. M. Trueblood, pp. 183–203.

organize "voluntary" and "productive" labor. At agreed-upon days (usually Sundays), local sectional CDR officials would send trucks or buses to the *reparto* to pick up volunteers to spend the day working in agricultural activities. It was, nevertheless, almost a year before CDRs were formed in Buena Ventura.

Background

The CDRs were formed following a speech by Fidel Castro on September 28, 1960, in which he called upon the Cuban people to establish a system of collective vigilance. Each street or block (in urban areas) would have a CDR whose primary duty would be to know who lived there, what they did, what their relations with the Batista government were, what kinds of things they were involved in, and with whom they met.[1] Thus, the founding of the CDRs was directly related to national security, and vigilance duties have remained a primary task of those organizations to this day.

As Castro asked in his rhetorical style on the twelfth anniversary of the CDRs, "Who can make a move without the CDRs knowing about it? Not even an ant! Why? Because there are four million activists." In the same speech Castro pointed out that although vigilance was the initial task of the CDRs, they went beyond that task long ago. Almost immediately these organizations were assigned numerous other duties, and they rapidly became the main vehicles for administration and political indoctrination at the local or "grass-roots" level.[2]

Unfortunately, most accounts about the CDRs have stressed almost exclusively the spying nature of the committees. For example, in an article entitled "Case Study of a Police State," Max Frankel of the *New York Times* talked of "the ugly emergence of neighborhood spies" and the appearance of concierges and janitors in government service "to report on the psychology as well as the physical conditions of tenants." Another *New York Times* writer, R. Hart Phillips, related that "to spy on one's neighbors and denounce them to the authorities is a 'patriotic duty'" and that Castro keeps his enemies under surveillance by the CDRs "which are composed of voluntary spies for the government."[3]

It is true that these articles appeared following the abortive Bay of Pigs invasion at a time when the Castro regime did employ repressive measures against its suspected enemies; nevertheless, a decade after the CDRs had ramified their interests to embrace activities as diverse as collecting old bottles and taking part in the Literacy Campaign, the press continued to view the committees as little more than spy rings. An article in the *Wall Street Journal* on the eve of the tenth anniversary of the establishment of the CDRs, while mentioning some of the multiple facets of these organizations, placed heavy emphasis on the vigilance functions of the committees; the article was entitled "Comrade Spy."[4]

Scholarly works on Cuba have, for the most part, been equally remiss in their coverage of the CDRs. Some do not even mention the committees, or, if they do, they usually dismiss the CDRs in cavalier fashion. Karol concludes that the CDRs "now have a purely repressive function."[5] Thomas' monumental study offers an exception to the neglect of the CDRs. His treatment of the committees is brief, but Thomas does not reduce them to mere spy organizations. In fact, he maintains that "these committees are really the core of the new Cuban society, creating a new culture of propaganda, participation, conformity and labour in a country which in the past was such a curious mixture of private endeavor and private suffering."[6]

The best and most comprehensive treatment of the CDRs to date has been by Fagen (1969). He concluded that the CDRs were the most far-reaching of all the mass organizations in Cuba. "One has only to compare the situation in 1960 with the situation eight years later," he pointed out, "to be convinced that the CDR have contributed very significantly to protecting the institutions and property of the revolution, to teaching citizens what is expected of them in the new Cuba, to mobilizing the population for participation in revolutionary activites, and to bringing together under a common organizational umbrella persons of the most diverse political and social characteristics."[7]

Operations of the CDRs

The first important undertaking of the CDRs followed the Bay of Pigs invasion of April, 1961. Fidel Castro called upon the committees to sort out potential counterrevolutionaries and denounce them to the appropriate authorities. Reports and eyewitness accounts leave no doubt that this operation was at best thorough and at worst overzealous in the extreme.[8] With the aid of the CDRs, perhaps one hundred thousand or more suspects were rounded up, and many of them were held incommunicado for days.[9] Castro himself admitted that injustices did occur, but he justified them on the grounds of national security.[10]

Nevertheless, the proposal put forth in the *New York Times* that "the mass arrests following the invasion brought a personal taste of terror to 1,000,000 Cubans" is hardly credible.[11]

Shortly after the Bay of Pigs invasion, it became necessary to ration lard and oil in Cuba. For this it was essential to know how many Cubans there were. A national census had not been taken since 1953, so the government considered it urgent to take another. There was no existing bureaucratic structure which could effectively do it on short notice, so the revolutionary regime turned to the CDRs.

Since each committee was supposed to have already taken a census of all residents in its block, it was relatively easy to use these figures for the new rationing program. Within twenty-two days the committees had enumerated six and one-half million Cubans.[12] The following year, when full-scale rationing began, Castro called upon the CDRs to cooperate with the Ministry of Commerce to issue and control the ration books.[13] In Havana alone, it was reported, the committees distributed 450,000 ration books in five days.[14]

Although they were still in an incipient stage of organization, the CDRs helped coordinate the Literacy Campaign of 1961. They were but one of the dozen or so organizations under the Comision Nacional de Alfabetización which participated in the campaign. But they were directly active in other areas of education. They tried to insure that children enrolled in school and attended regularly. If there were problems along these lines, CDR representatives visited the children's parents. They sorted out exemplary students and "exemplary parents" and recruited thousands of people to help in adult education.[15]

Whenever possible, political study groups were organized by the CDRs. These groups met once a month and, in the early 1970's, were attended by some two million people.[16] Some instructors in these study circles were trained in special cadre schools of political indoctrination. The cadre schools (Escuelas de Cuadros de los CDRs) were established following a speech by Fidel Castro commemorating the second anniversary of the founding of the CDRs.[17]

The committees played a key role in public health programs. They operated People's Schools of Public Health, giving instruction in sanitation, first aid, and trash disposal. They were also instrumental in the national polio immunization campaign in which over two million children were vaccinated. The campaign eliminated polio from the island; a similar effort has practically eliminated tuberculosis.

Although yellow fever had ceased to exist in Cuba, the committees were instructed to direct programs of eradication of the mosquito which carried the disease. Collaborating with the Ministry of Public Health, the CDRs undertook campaigns to encourage women to submit to cytological tests in order to detect uterine cancer. They also urged and organized citizens to donate blood for local and international needs. After the earthquake in Peru in 1970, the CDRs collected one hundred thousand donations in just ten days.[18]

Like many other voluntary organizations, the committees adopted "emulation campaign" techniques. CDR officials helped encourage laborers in work centers (*centros de trabajo*) to outdo each other, "emulate" the best performers, and set an example for others. Outstanding workers were distinguished as "vanguard workers" (*obreros vanguardias*) and were honored in national ceremonies.[19] With the assistance of the work centers, the CDRs organized voluntary labor projects—unpaid labor performed beyond regular working hours.[20]

During the 1970 sugar harvest the CDRs were extremely active to prevent sabotage and report failure of workers to perform as they should. They cooperated closely with the Ministry of the Interior and the armed forces in that job as well as in guarding state property and frontier areas against invasion.[21]

The committees were intimately involved with the functioning of the People's Courts. CDR officials could make up a list of nominations for judges, help collect evidence, and sometimes serve as witnesses during the trials.[22] The CDRs also worked with the organs of Poder Local (Local Power) and later with Poder Popular (People's Power).[23]

A major task of the CDRs was the collection of raw materials for reuse or reprocessing by government industry. Old bottles, newspapers and cardboard, scrap metal, and other materials collected by volunteers were sent by the committees to one of the processing plants of the Empresa Consolidada de Recuperación de Materias Primas (Consolidated Enterprise for the Recovery of Raw Materials). In 1972 alone the CDRs collected 88 million glass containers of various kinds and thirty thousand tons of raw materials for the paper industry. The Cuban government estimated that from the time of organization of the CDRs in 1960 to early 1972, the CDRs had saved Cuba more than 17 million pesos through their campaigns to collect raw materials.[24]

In summary, despite these activities, the primary task of the CDRs remained vigilance. Booth thought the reasons for this were twofold: "Firstly, enemies of the revolution in the strict sense of saboteurs and anti-communist guerilla contingents still made their appearance from time to time during the late 'sixties, as they have continued to do since, though nearly always from abroad. Secondly, and more significantly, the focus of CDR "vigilance" proper had broadened and shifted decisively, being now concerned almost exclusively with combatting common crime."[25]

Organization of the CDRs

The Committees for the Defense of the Revolution were organized hierarchically in pyramidal form.[26] Until 1966 there were at the bottom the neighborhood, block, or base committees. Each block or its equivalent had a CDR with locally elected officials. Immediately above the block level were the zone and sectional CDRs. The zone and sectional committees had the responsibility of "orienting" the block CDRs (mainly providing political education and indoctrination), assigning them specific tasks, and reviewing complaints and recommendations of the base-level organizations. Sectional CDRs generally comprised no more than twenty block CDRs, and in rural areas of dispersed population they included as few as seven base-level organizations.[27]

In 1966 the intermediate-level organs of the CDRs were reorganized to bring them into line with new jurisdictional units introduced in local government during that year. These provided for the first time a uniform division of the country to be observed by most state agencies and political organizations. Under the new system, urban "sections" corresponded to "municipalities" (*municipios*) in rural areas, and each was responsible for coordinating the work of a number of constituent "zones."[28]

Higher up there were six provincial committees, one for each province in the nation and one for the Isle of Youth (Pines). Finally, there was the National Directorate of Committees for the Defense of the Revolution, under the Central Committee of the Communist Party, with administrative control over all the levels below it.

Initiative was encouraged at the "grass-roots" levels—the block, zone, and sectional CDRs. The higher levels preferred to limit their direction to major policy decisions. The neighborhood and zonal committees were run by elected citizens who did not receive pay for the CDR work. The higher organs in the system were staffed by full-time, salaried workers.[29]

There were as many as sixteen officers at the block level heading different "fronts."[30] At a minimum there would usually be a president and officers in charge of vigilance, finances, public health, and voluntary labor. Frequently there were also "fronts" of education, organization, supplies, propaganda and culture, and sports and recreation.

Ideally, block meetings were held once a week, but they often convened less frequently. Officers were expected to attend all meetings, which were usually held late in the evening, and members of the organization were urged to attend. At the meetings, problems of the block or neighborhood were discussed, and needs and recommendations were forwarded to the zone or sectional committee. The meetings also served as clearinghouses for policies and propaganda handed down from the upper levels.

Membership in the CDRs was voluntary, but everyone over fourteen years of age was encouraged to join. Token dues were collected monthly from each member, the amount depending on whether a person worked for wages or not. A percentage of the receipts was employed by the block CDRs for local expenditures, and the remainder was forwarded to the next higher level.

By 1977 the CDRs were reported to have nearly five million members, about half the total Cuban population.[31]

Buena Ventura and the CDRs

The sectional committee responsible for Buena Ventura set up four CDRs in the housing project, one for each block. However, confusion and ignorance surrounded the organization of the committees, and, despite good intentions by the sectional CDR, communication and understanding between the new housing project representatives and the sectional directors were at a minimum. No records were kept by the Buena Ventura CDRs; as a consequence, today few agree upon or remember details of the early days of the committees in Buena Ventura.

Elections were only nominally democratic, and just a few of the offices or "fronts" were filled by popular vote. Other officers were named by the sectional committee without consulting the residents of

Buena Ventura. Some offices remained vacant. A few influential individuals in each block had their views prevail, though more by default than by coercion. They did, however, operate to insure that the most important posts were taken by themselves or their hand-picked followers.

In view of the confusion and conflict surrounding the formation of the CDRs in Buena Ventura, it is surprising that the committees functioned there at all. Yet they achieved, albeit in a somewhat limited way, a number of the goals set by themselves and by the upper echelons.

It became apparent very early that one of the blocks, designed largely for single elderly people, could not support its own CDR. The initial recruiting drive succeeded in registering only five members of the block, the youngest of whom was sixty-four years of age. Three of these recruits became officers. However, the president of the committee moved from Buena Ventura, and his replacement went to work permanently in agriculture, leaving only three members and no president. As a result, this CDR merged with a neighboring one.

With the new structure of three CDRs in the four blocks, the committees introduced nightly vigilance in the housing project. Guard duty was kept from midnight to dawn. Usually there were two shifts: a pair of women kept guard from midnight to 2:30 A.M. and were replaced by a couple of men until dawn. Those on guard duty were not permitted to carry fire-arms. Although this denial of arms to the guards was not unusual, the people of Buena Ventura resented it, considering it another indication that government officials would never trust former inhabitants of Las Yaguas.

The CDRs in Buena Ventura seem to have reached their peak of efficiency in 1965, a year after their formation. This is not to say that they were ever very efficient or carried out tasks to a degree that the revolutionary government ever cited them as "exemplary CDRs." But to paraphrase Fagen in his resumé of CDR operations in the nation, despite evidence of disorganization and incompetence, in the main suspects did get reported, children did get vaccinated, consumers did get counted, and evening classes did get taught.[32] It would be difficult to imagine that any of these tasks would have been handled nearly as well without the CDRs.

About 1966 the CDRs in Buena Ventura began to cease to function, and by the time of our study they had become completely paralyzed.

The fronts still existed in name, and most of the old officers retained their titular positions, but not a single task was being performed. All guard duty had stopped; public health, recuperation of raw materials, and other campaigns had long since ceased to be undertaken; block meetings were no longer held, and local CDR officers did not attend the sectional meetings. And at a time when the Cuban nation was emotionally and economically geared to reach its goal of harvesting ten million tons of sugarcane, only a scattering of individuals from the housing project turned out sporadically for voluntary labor.[33]

Nicolás Salazar, a block CDR official in Buena Ventura, related to us: "The CDR stopped functioning in the *barrio* in 1968. People began to lose their will to work. When we did anything at all, it was something easy. We got a directive from the sectional to collect bottles, perfume containers, silver coins, and canceled stamps. Enrique Cueva and I collected four sackfuls of containers from the neighbors. We did it against Minerva's will.[34] She said we couldn't carry out a task without consulting her first. But she was ailing and hardly ever wanted to work for the committee."[35]

Nicolás pointed up one of the reasons for the demise of the CDRs in Buena Ventura: sheer inertia or laziness. But there were other, interdependent, factors. For one thing, personal feuds and animosities, which always had put a brake on proper CDR functioning in the housing settlement, eventually became incompatible with effective action on the part of the committees. For another, there was a total breakdown in communication and cooperation between Buena Ventura and the sectional committee. Nicolás Salazar continues:

Last year I went to the sectional to talk with Comrade Lina. "Look, Lina," I said, "we need you to come down and hold a meeting with all the neighbors to get the CDR going. It's stalled."

"Comrade," she answered, "this is a problem without a solution. We've gone there several times to hold meetings. But nobody comes. We send down directives and they don't carry out the tasks. If people hang back and don't do the work, what can we do?"

She's decided we're incorrigible and dropped us. Well, I must admit she's right. I remember that at the beginning of 1969 a woman comrade came down to make [sic] a census about who was doing guard duty. The comrade in charge of Vigilance had to sign it, but nobody could be found to take on the responsibility. Even the president and the organizer refused to sign, according to Lina. After that she stopped sending down directives or anybody to help us.[36]

As the sectional committee grew increasingly unresponsive, complaints arose in the housing project, and eventually resignation set in.
CDR President Abelardo Fuentes commented:

> This sectional committee we have isn't worth a cent. They say dirty
> things, obscene things—that we used to live in Las Yaguas, that we're
> thieves and the women here are prostitutes. The sectional president is the
> one who has run down this neighborhood in every way, and she even
> had the nerve to accuse me, a man who's never set foot in a police
> station in my life and never had a brush with the law, of the worst things
> you can think of. She went so far as to say that we're a bunch of crooks
> in Buena Ventura. She said *that* because we live in such a poor
> neighborhood. This place is excluded from all organizations, from
> everything. When you get right down to it I don't care what happens any
> more. I'm sixty years old and have lived long enough.

Why did the sectional cease to give aid and instruction to the
committees of Buena Ventura? One reason was that it believed that it
had done its best with the available resources. The people had gotten
their new homes, and most of the men were employed. The sectional
had subordinated other tasks to devote a large amount of time and
energy to rehabilitating the former slum dwellers and indoctrinating
them with revolutionary ideals. After several years of this work, the
sectional believed that even though it had an ongoing commitment to
Buena Ventura, it had to divert its energies into other things, especially
in 1969–70 to the sugarcane harvest.

Beyond this, sectional officials had become disheartened at the lack
of progress in Buena Ventura. They felt they had done their best, and
as tasks increasingly went undone in the housing project, the sectional
eventually stopped assigning them. As for the people of Buena
Ventura, they interpreted the actions, or want of them, on the part of
the sectional as one more indication that people from Las Yaguas were
simply not worth bothering with.

Underlying these reasons for the failure of the CDRs in Buena
Ventura was the large cultural gap between the former residents of Las
Yaguas and the people with whom they had to interact—their
neighbors, the sectional officials, and, on occasion, higher echelon
bureaucrats. "The people from below" were never allowed to forget
their origins. One woman residing in the middle-class neighborbood
above the housing project told us: "I've lived here since 1967. When I
arrived those people were already here, but we didn't know about them

at first. We still have very little contact with them, only in the store. Just imagine the impact! Their educational level is so low. They feel discriminated against, and when you mention Las Yaguas to them, they jump. For that reason, I never mention it."

Through a combination of revolutionary zeal, pressure from above, and a desire to form a viable community, most people in Buena Ventura seem to have tried to forget their rivalries and to prevent new ones from emerging. A supposedly democratic, egalitarian organization like the CDR, in which everyone would have an equal voice in the future of his community, seemed an ideal structure to alleviate friction. Ultimately, almost the opposite appeared to have happened. The dilemma was expressed by Lucía Martínez, the mother-in-law of one of the CDR presidents:

> I don't know why, but now my old friends and I don't visit each other anymore. I ask myself if something has happened here to make the people so distant. I don't know if it's the committee, but many people don't treat you as they did before. People here get along worse than when we lived in Las Yaguas. After they installed the CDR here everybody turned their backs on us. Your closest neighbors are those who are the most remote. I believe that it's because almost everyone here has something up his sleeve, so he doesn't want to have friends or visitors. And the best way to hide what they're up to is to withdraw and not allow visitors so they can't see what's going on. Everybody's afraid, and since they don't want to find out what's going on, they turn their backs on us.

To conclude, the Committees for the Defense of the Revolution in Buena Ventura experienced a limited degree of success for a year or so after their founding but gradually became paralyzed. I do not claim that Buena Ventura is a typical case.[37] Indeed, the record offers us some striking successes elsewhere. The Cuban government has published numerous accounts of committees that function at a high degree of efficiency.[38] Most of these reports have a Pollyannic quality about them, but outside observers such as José Yglesias (1968) leave little doubt that many CDRs have performed remarkable tasks. However, there were, at least in the 1960's and early 1970's, common problems surrounding the committees, whether they were located in Buena Ventura or elsewhere. Fagen expressed it well:

> Among the problems associated with the performance of the CDR, one stands out above all others: the cost to the legitimacy of the revolution.

The committees have been plagued from the beginning by various forms of arbitrary, officious, self-serving, and corrupt behavior on the part of some of their members, behavior that has cost the revolution dearly in the coin of support and thus of legitimacy. Many citizens' most direct and frequent contact with any revolutionary institution is with the local committee; and when committee members are arbitrary, uninformed, opportunistic, or corrupt, the popular image of the revolutionary movement suffers accordingly.[39]

Notes

1. Fidel Castro, *Discursos de Fidel en los Aniversarios de los CDR 1960–1967*, p. 17. Castro's call for the CDRs was supposedly a spontaneous reaction to the explosion of several petards during his speech. However, some months before, he had spoken of the need for increased vigilance and formation of civil defense teams (see Richard R. Fagen, *The Transformation of Political Culture in Cuba*, pp. 69–70).

2. *Granma*, October 8, 1972, p. 2. José Matar, first coordinator of the National Directorate of the CDRs (later expelled from the Communist party) insisted that it would be a mistake to think of the CDR system as an administrative appendage of the government. He said that the CDRs are, above all, political and social (or politicizing and socializing) organizations. "The CDRs are inculcating in hundreds of thousands of their members a feeling of civic responsibility toward the Fatherland, a feeling that the apparatus of the state is not abstract and distant, but close and respected, because it is *their* state" (quoted in Richard R. Fagen, *The Transformation of Political Culture in Cuba*, p. 86).

3. "Case Study of a Police State," *New York Times Magazine*, April 30, 1961, p. 88.

4. "Comrade Spy: How a Cuban Worker Helps Keep 'Revolution' Alive," *Wall Street Journal*, August 20, 1970, p. 15. Vigilance has remained a primary concern of the CDRs.

5. K. S. Karol, *Guerrillas in Power: The Course of the Cuban Revolution*, p. 457.

6. Hugh Thomas, *Cuba: The Pursuit of Freedom*, p. 1457.

7. Fagen, *Transformation of Political Culture*, pp. 99–100.

8. Lee Lockwood comments: "Many [prisoners], it appears, were the victims of overzealous revolutionary tribunals which, in the aftermath of the Bay of Pigs invasion, meted out justice with a vindictive severity reminiscent of the Reign of Terror in revolutionary France" (*Castro's Cuba; Cuba's Fidel*, p. 248).

9. Estimates of the number of people apprehended at this time vary. Fagen, *Transformation of Political Culture*, p. 73, says that by April 19 tens of thousands had been detained. He adds that the total number was probably in excess of one hundred thousand and cites an estimate of two hundred thousand by an Italian journalist. Thomas says, "Between the raids on 15 April and the evening of 17 April, perhaps 100,000 were arrested, including all the bishops . . . many journalists and the vast majority of the real underground, including most of the CIA's 2,500 agents and their 20,000 suspected counter-revolutionary sympathizers" (*Cuba*, p. 1365).

10. *Revolución*, April 24, 1961, p. 11.

11. *New York Times*, June 12, 1961, p. 1. This estimate is based on the assumption that each of two hundred thousand Cubans arrested had an average of four close relatives who were affected.

12. Cuba, Dirección Nacional de los CDR, *Pueblo organizado*, p. 12.
13. *Obra Revolucionaria*, no. 7 (March 14, 1962), p. 24.
14. Dirección Nacional de los CDR, *Pueblo Organizado*, p. 13.
15. *Granma*, October 8, 1972, p. 2.
16. *Ibid.*
17. Castro, *Discursos*, p. 76.
18. Howard I. Blutstein et al., *Area Handbook for Cuba*; Dirección Nacional de los CDR, *Pueblo organizado*, p. 13; *Granma*, October 8, 1972, p. 2; *Bohemia*, July 5, 1968. (suppl.), p. 112; June 26, 1970, p. 68.
19. Work center CDR committees were dissolved in 1967, and their memberships were transferred to their block CDRs, thus eliminating dual membership (David Booth, "Neighbourhood Committees and Popular Courts in the Social Transformation of Cuba" [Ph.D. diss., University of Surrey, 1973]). Nevertheless, emulation in work centers went on.
20. *Bohemia*, March 27, 1970, pp. 64–65; Dirección Nacional de los CDR, *Pueblo organizado*, p. 13. Unpaid labor was also supplied by unemployed women, students, prisoners, and military recruits (see Carmelo Mesa-Lago, "Economic Significance of Unpaid Labor in Socialist Cuba," *Industrial and Labor Relations Review* 22 [1969]: 354).
21. Lowry Nelson, *Rural Cuba*, p. 179.
22. J. Berman, "The Cuban Popular Tribunals," *Columbia Law Review* 69 (1969): 1317–54.
23. Local Power was an attempt to involve people in "policing" their own neighborhoods—that is, cleaning streets and the like. People's Power is a system of popularly elected administrative and legislative assemblies. Its aim is to transfer administrative/legislative functions from state agencies to the provinces. It went into effect some years after our study.
24. *Granma*, October 8, 1972, pp. 2, 11.
25. Booth, "Neighbourhood Committees," p. 58. The second reason seems overstated, since his closing speech to the First Congress of the Committees for the Defense of the Revolution in 1977, Fidel Castro noted that the Congress stressed the need to fight "common crime" as well as political crime (*Granma*, October 8, 1972, p. 3).
26. For details of the organization of the CDRs the reader is referred to Fagen, *Transformation of Political Culture*, and Booth, "Neighbourhood Committees."
27. Cuba, Dirección Nacional de los CDR, *Los CDR en granjas y zonas rurales*, p. 11.
28. Booth, "Neighbourhood Committees," pp. 42–44.
29. Direct from Cuba, *Committees for the Defense of the Revolution*, n.d., p. 4.
30. Fronts (*frentes*) were areas of responsibility.
31. *Granma Weekly Review*, October 9, 1977, p. 5.
32. Fagen, *Transformation of Political Culture*, p. 98.
33. Booth notes that 1970 was a very bad year for the CDRs. "During the first part of 1970 the committees were subject to neglect—reflected in the zero growth of their membership—due to single-mindedness with which Cubans participated in the sugar harvest 'of the Ten Million tons'" (Booth, "Neighbourhood Committees," p. 63).
34. Minerva Ruz was organizer of the CDR to which Nicolás belonged. The post was not one of the highest in the hierarchy of the committee, but Minerva was one of those people who worked behind the scenes to get her way. She was a strong-willed woman, accused by some of using her powers to cover up misdeeds by her family and friends. Her powers were religious, personal, and political, more or less in that order.

Her religious influence was gained through *santería* practices learned from her mother (a powerful *santera* in Las Yaguas) and involved witchcraft or black magic.

35. Oscar Lewis, Ruth M. Lewis, and Susan M. Rigdon, *Four Men: Living the Revolution: An Oral History of Contemporary Cuba*, p. 400.

36. *Ibid.*

37. We made cursory investigations of the CDRs in the other housing projects where Las Yaguas residents had been resettled. In general it seems that they experienced the same initial successes and suffered the same decay as the committees in Buena Ventura.

38. See, for example, Dirección Nacional de los CDR, *Los CDR* and *Pueblo organizado*, and issues of *Bohemia*, *Con la Guardia en Alto*, and *Revolución*. See also Butterworth, "Grass-Roots Political Organization."

39. Fagen, *Transformation of Political Culture*, p. 100.

8

People's Courts

Trials in People's Courts for the residents of Buena Ventura were usually held in a store building about a mile from the housing development. The store also served as headquarters for the sectional CDR. Judges serving a particular locality were selected from among its residents and the court hearings held there.[1] However, no people's judges had been selected from the Buena Ventura housing project, nor were any trials held there.

In order to observe the implementation of popular justice, our staff attended and tape-recorded six sessions, during which at least fourteen different cases were heard, some involving people from the housing project. One of these trials is summarized in this chapter.[2]

Background

People's Courts were originally conceived by Fidel Castro in the early 1960's to provide legal services for rural areas in Cuba.[3] They were not established in the nation's capital until 1966, although three experimental courts were set up outside Havana in the Mayabeque Region in 1963. By the time of our study in 1969–70, judges in these courts heard cases in nearly every residential neighborhood throughout Cuba.

Each section had its own People's Court, which had jurisdiction over twenty to thirty square blocks in urban areas. Sections had as many as forty judges available, but only three sat at any one session.

Theodore MacDonald, Jr., is author of the major part of this chapter.

Sometimes these trios were firmly set to work together and sometimes not, but they were supposed to rotate offices during the trial sessions.

Superseding the previous Correctional Courts (one-man tribunals whose decisions were, in practice, not subject to appeal), the three-judge People's Courts presided over cases usually involving civil suits, certain misdemeanors, health and sanitary violations, juvenile delinquency, drunkenness, and personal quarrels, but their competence also extended to larceny and assault.[4]

People's Court cases could be initiated in any one of four ways: by private citizens, the CDRs, the police, or, in cases of perjury or contempt, the courts themselves. In the first three instances, a written accusation had to be dictated at the local police station and then lodged at the offices of the court.[5]

In addition to such jurisprudential goals as resolving disputes and discouraging "antisocial behavior," people's judges consistently emphasized a concern for constructive and rehabilitative sanctions, public participation, and "popular education." Setting up courts in store buildings or even out on the street, the judges were taught to exercise informal, democratic, and personal social control, guided by instructions to educate and integrate offenders rather than to castigate them.

Thus, by installing locally elected, nonprofessional judges in a court with considerable local autonomy and public participation, the Cuban government attempted to carry out its goals to decrease the alienation and opposition which often existed between the people and the courts, increase participation in the revolutionary process, and, at the same time, encourage acceptance of Cuban law.

People's judges were laymen, not professional elites, and peers of the litigants. Judicial candidates needed only to be over twenty-one years of age, good workers, and respected by their neighbors and to have completed six years of elementary school. There was also an unspecified requirement that potential judges be "revolutionaries." Our data reveal that, except for the last, some of these requirements were occasionally waived.

The courts were under the jurisdiction of the Ministry of Justice; however, they maintained considerable independence and local autonomy, which encouraged a potentially high degree of popular participation. According to Blas Roca, then president of the Commission for Constitutional Studies, a degree of self-government and local representation in the courts allowed the people to realize that the courts were not "something official, something which comes down from above, something alien to them."[6]

The Ministry of Justice directed the sectional CDR unit to provide a certain number of candidates for judges. The CDR, in cooperation with the Communist party, then was supposed to call for an open assembly in which candidates were nominated and elected by the audience. It was apparent, however, that in Buena Ventura spontaneous election by the masses was infrequent. Before the public assembly, the CDR and party members met to prepare a list of acceptable candidates who were nominated by members of these organizations.[7] They stated that if nominations were spontaneous, few of those selected by the masses would meet the requirements, and there would not be enough judges to fulfill the quotas set by the Ministry of Justice.

In any event, the selected judicial candidates would attend a training period varying from seven to fourteen days, during which instructors from the Ministry of Justice taught the candidates Cuban law, took them to observe trials in existing People's Courts, helped them perform mock trials, and, finally, examined them on what they had absorbed during the training period. At the same time, the Communist party conducted an intensive investigation and evaluation of the candidates to be certain their backgrounds, attitudes, and behavior did not conflict with the goals of the Revolution.

Candidates who successfully completed the training and passed investigation were again presented before a public assembly for final ratification. Those who were approved continued judicial training for an additional period. At that time they were provided with a judge's manual which outlined uniform procedures, exemplary cases, and appropriate sanctions.[8] Although the formal training and procedures were considered important, one of the people's judges whom our staff interviewed said, "What is uppermost is to impart justice which goes beyond what is written on paper." Consequently, during the training, and later in practice, the judges were encouraged to deemphasize formal legal procedures and standardized sanctions in favor of more personal and rehabilitative treatment, including consideration of the defendant's past criminal record, personal and family needs, health, and employment.

With rehabilitative considerations in mind, the judges frequently handed down suspended sentences in which the guilty party or parties might be sentenced but not required to fulfill the sanction on condition that they not appear before the courts during a specified period of time. This was done in the hope that the suspended sentence would give the defendant a chance to mend his or her ways and develop into a more cooperative, "social-minded" person.

Buena Ventura and the People's Courts

Insofar as the residents of Buena Ventura were concerned, our investigation indicated that when sentences were actually enforced, a frequent requirement was that the sanctioned party or parties attend a number of "study circles." One of the judges serving Buena Ventura explained that the purpose of these circles was to get the convicted person to understand the significance of his infraction by discussing both the nature of his antisocial behavior as defined by the new Cuban society and the duties of a Cuban citizen. The convicted person fulfilled his sanction over a period of time by attending classes usually held in the evenings. This particular judge claimed that after they had completed their sanction, many people continued to attend the circle.

Productive labor, generally agricultural work, was a common penalty handed down by the courts. In many cases the sanction consisted of only a warning designed to discourage continued practice of minor offenses. Even the most severe sanction—temporary deprivation of liberty—was regarded as rehabilitative.[9]

Regardless of the severity of the sanction, every sentence was administered with a lengthy reprimand which allowed the judge to explain the concept of "antisocial behavior" as defined by the new Cuban society and also outline the goals of the People's Courts.

Before each trial began, the judges were expected to go into the litigants' neighborhood (which might well be the same as their own) and solicit comments and information concerning the upcoming case, hopefully enabling them to evaluate the individuals involved and evidence to be presented.[10]

Before each case was heard, the accused was supposed to be advised of his rights. He could reject any one, or all, of the judges on the grounds of personal enmity, friendship, or kinship; he could elect to be defended by a third person, lay or professional; and, after the hearing, he could appeal to a special court composed of two different judges together with an assessor of the municipality. According to Booth, in Havana in 1969, it was seldom that the accused availed himself of his first two rights, but appeals were frequent in the more serious cases.[11] In Buena Ventura there were complaints that defendants were not told of their right to appeal. During the public trial which followed the investigation, spontaneous testimony was allowed from the audience, and the tribunal could solicit additional testimony from the spectators before deliberation.[12]

As mentioned, the People's Courts sought to function as an educational forum. One judge explained that this was essential in Buena Ventura since the majority of those from the housing project who appeared before the People's Courts were apathetic toward the Revolution. The judge said that the courts tried to get them involved in the Revolution and that, in this sense, the courts were like schools for the Buena Venturans.

In this respect the People's Courts were attempting to help mold the "New Cuban Man"—a creative, cooperative, and active citizen. As Fagen explained: "The transformation of Cuban man into revolutionary man is at the heart of Cuban radicalism: it is seen by the leadership as a requisite for the success of the new institutional order. . . . In the Cuban view, there is no successful or lasting Leninist politics, agrarian reform, economic transformations, or international realignments without the education of the Cuban masses."[13] Che Guevara wrote that this integrative and educational process was two-sided: "On the one side, society acts through direct and indirect education; on the other, the individual subjects himself to a process of conscious self-education."[14]

The Trial

In the case discussed here, the tribunal was composed of Tomás Martínez, Roberto Fernández, and Ana Pérez.[15] They all lived in a socioeconomically mixed neighborhood not far from Buena Ventura.

Tomás Martínez was a sixty-year-old retired teacher with a degree in education from the University of Havana. He helped to establish some of the first CDRs in the nation's capital and was among the first to be selected as a judge when the People's Courts were formed in the locality which included Buena Ventura.

Roberto Fernández fifty-two years of age, was born in Havana and had only a fifth-grade education. He had been elected president of his local CDR and headed several other neighborhood organizations.

In 1969, bypassing the public assembly, the local CDR and the Communist party nominated him to attend judicial training school.

The third member of the tribunal was forty-four-year-old Ana Pérez. Born and raised in Havana, she attended school for seven years until her father died and she was forced to take care of the household while her mother worked. As with the other two judges, the coming of the Revolution drew her into community activities. During the initial public assembly for the selection of judicial candidates in her locality, she was nominated by a woman in the audience. After some initial hesitation, she accepted. Subsequently, in addition to being a judge, she became an instructor of new judges and president of the judges in her locality.

In contrast to the judges, the litigants had not been drawn into active participation in the revolutionary process. The plaintiff, Jacinto Varona, was a black, sixty-six-year-old janitor in a medical clinic. One of eight children from a tenant-farming family in Oriente Province, Jacinto never attended school and left home early to work as an itinerant farmhand. In the 1940's he drifted into Havana and began selling perfume on the streets. Later he moved into the house of a friend in Las Yaguas, where he and the friend opened up a small and unsuccessful kiosk.

Following the triumph of the Revolution, Jacinto attended literacy classes for a time, but, as he claimed, because of his poor vision he was unable to progress and dropped the classes. He had not taken part in any neighborhood revolutionary organizations.

Jacinto's common-law wife, twenty-nine-year-old Panchita Saenz, was the defendant. She was a mulatto, born in Oriente Province as well. She never attended school regularly until after the Revolution, when she completed the fourth grade. At the age of fourteen she married a coffee grower in the province. It was an unhappy marriage and, after giving birth to three children, she left her husband.

Panchita met Jacinto in 1963. At that time Jacinto was working on the construction of the Buena Ventura housing project. Jacinto felt the need for a wife and sent a request to a friend in Oriente. Panchita had been living alone and, since Jacinto had a house, she accepted his offer sight unseen. After living in Las Yaguas for a short while, the couple moved to Buena Ventura. They had three children together.

About a year before our study, Jacinto and Panchita became estranged. Jacinto slept by himself in one of the three bedrooms in their house, Panchita and her five daughters slept in another, and her fifteen-year-old son in the third. She allowed her relatives the use of her son's bedroom when they were in town.

Although Pancihta did not participate in any political activities or belong to any voluntary associations, she told our staff that she regarded herself as a revolutionary. Her attitude was probably influenced by the activities of her brother and grandfather, who fought with Fidel Castro in the Sierra Maestra. She was highly critical of her neighbors in this report: "I don't see any 'New Man' in this housing project. If their parents had been different, these kids might become something. But if they keep growing up the way they are now, they'll turn out just like the rest of them, sticking their noses in where they don't belong and bumming around like thieves. They'll go to jail, get out in two or three months, and be right back in again. They have no respect for their mothers or anything else that would make them good revolutionaries. They'll never make anything of themselves."

Panchita and Jacinto had been to court several times since their estrangement. Three months before the case reviewed here, Jacinto had brought action against Panchita and one of her daughters, claiming that they had attacked him with clubs without cause. He stated that they had been having arguments ever since he caught her embracing an ambulance driver in their patio a few weeks before the attack. A short time later Panchita accused Jacinto of stealing her suitcase. No sanctions other than warnings were administered in those cases.

Jacinto brought action against Panchita once again in October, 1969. He told the court he arrived home to see Panchita in her bedroom with a man, Cheo González, and with the latches drawn on the two doors. He said he then went to fetch a policeman. Panchita said that Cheo was a relative serving in the army who slept at her home every time he had a pass. She claimed that Jacinto wanted her out of the house and that he slandered her to achieve his ends. She added that this was not the first time he had attempted to defame her character and demanded that the proceedings be postponed until Cheo could be brought in as a witness. The judge agreed.

Cheo corroborated Panchita's testimony and stated that he had always behaved himself properly when staying with Panchita and had no other relationship with her than that of a sincere friendship.

Judge Pérez, who was acting as recording secretary that evening, announced to the audience that the People's Courts normally did not penalize or even consider cases involving a woman's deception of her husband. She told Cheo that he had been summoned only because

Panchita requested his presence to vindicate her reputation. Further, she added, if this had been the first complaint involving Panchita and Jacinto, the judges would simply have filed it away. Jacinto objected to the proceedings on the basis that a policeman and a CDR official whom he had sought out to verify what he had allegedly seen were not in court.

The trial, however, did proceed, and, following testimony by Jacinto and Panchita's brother Ernesto, the judges' panel deliberated and decided that the charges against Panchita were to be dismissed. Jacinto was given a suspended sentence of sixty days on a work farm on condition that he not pester or calumniate Panchita. Panchita was warned against provoking Jacinto. Both the plaintiff and the defendant were given reprimands by Judge Pérez and sanctioned to attend evening study circles.

The case presented here may not have been typical of People's Trials, and we do not pretend to offer it as a basis for generalization. Nevertheless, it does illustrate some of the successes and failures of People's Courts—at least of the one that served Buena Ventura.

On the positive side, the proliferation of neighborhood courts resulted in a more rapid processing of cases. Before the People's Courts, complaints often waited for a year or more before being adjudicated. After the courts were instituted, cases were usually heard within a month after they were registered. In addition to providing more rapid resolution of conflicts, easy access to the courts encouraged more frequent use of their services. One of the judges interviewed for this study commented, "Before the People's Courts arrived, many problems were not brought out into the open. People never bothered to file complaints. Consequently, their tensions kept festering until they finally came to a head in more serious crimes. Now people know their complaints will be taken care of more quickly, and they are more likely to ask the courts to intervene." As a result, although the number of courts has increased, so have the cases. The judges were able to continue processing cases rapidly by holding court frequently (several times a week), although they predicted that many more judges would eventually be needed.

Despite being overburdened, the members of the tribunal maintained a personal concern for each of the litigants and were allowed considerable latitude and freedom. They utilized this freedom to tailor sanctions especially suitable to the needs of the litigants. In the case of

Panchita and Jacinto, both were given evening and weekend sanctions requiring productive labor in the neighborhood, thus allowing them to continue to work and to care for their children.

In a negative respect, there was little demand for first-hand evidence and proven guilt in the Saenz-Varona trials. A similar failure to observe procedural guarantees was evident when the judges failed to summon crucial wittnesses—the policeman and the CDR official—for Jacinto's defense. At the time, Jacinto was more concerned with the problem of hearsay evidence than were the judges. Apparently, although a number of guarantees were written into the Social Defense Code, which helped guide the Popular Courts, their application was inconsistent.

Other problems of the People's Courts became evident during this study. For example, it was often out of the hands of the courts to resolve a conflict. All three judges agreed that Jacinto and Panchita should live apart, but the housing shortage in Cuba made separate residences impossible. Consequently, two angry, volatile people were forced to continue living together and were sanctioned for not doing so peacefully.

The failure of the litigants to carry out the sentences illustrates another problem mentioned by each judge: the difficulty of enforcing sanctions. Jacinto simply ignored his and Panchita maneuvered out of hers. Persistent follow-up might have helped to eliminate problems such as Jacinto's, but in Panchita's case the judges lamented that there were not enough day-care centers for children whose parents should serve sentence during the day. There were also insufficient resources to support a sanctioned person's family while he served an extended sentence away from home. Not until the Cuban government can resolve these needs will the courts be able to sanction more effectively.

There were other stumbling blocks to popular justice in Buena Ventura. Although contrary to official policy, both spatial and social distance separated the residents of the housing development from the judges. The judges in the cases witnessed by our staff were more educated and better off economically than most of the litigants. In addition, although none of the judges lived in Buena Ventura, the majority of the cases brought before them involved residents of that neighborhood.

However well-meaning the judges were, their "middle-class morality" frequently alienated the people, thereby prejudicing the efforts of the courts to integrate them into the new Cuban society and to educate them to its goals. This middle-class morality came out clearly during and after the recorded trial of Panchita Saenz and Jacinto Varona. Judge Pérez told members of the staff: "I understand that among those people of low culture, morality doesn't count much. They don't even keep their children from seeing such things. They let their desires free and bring their lovers home with perfect ease. We think that's a poor way to rear children. That's my opinion."

Ana Pérez, who did most of the questioning during the Saenz-Varona trial, appeared to have difficulties separating her opinions from that of the court as a body. For example, she said to Jacinto during the trial: "This court doesn't think it was necessary for you to call the police to speak with this man [Cheo] who had been in your house so long and had enjoyed your friendship. You stood to ruin not only your wife but also the man you had previously trusted. We don't think you acted as a real man should."

There was also the problem of sympathies or hostilities directed at those involved in the trial by the judges, with a hint of sexism involved. Judge Pérez, for example, told the Court (referring to Jacinto Varona), "It's not logical for a man to keep on repeating day after day that his wife has a lover. . . . If he thinks his wife has been unfaithful, he should stop pestering her and simply leave her."

Along these lines, Judge Tomás Martínez, in discussing the Saenz-Varona case with our staff, said: "I have a feeling that Saenz is not a bad person. I think she must be understood according to the surrounding she comes from, where her whole personality developed. She's a tyrannical, violent, and unsociable woman, even though she is more educated than her husband. . . . In the neighborhood they say there is a certain promiscuity in her life and men go there frequently."

We raised the problem of lack of peer representation on the bench to one of the regional court advisors. He considered that although many of the former residents of Las Yaguas had enough education (six years) to qualify as judges, their attitude toward the rest of society often rendered them incapable of serving in that capacity. He explained: "In pre-Revolutionary Cuba there was a great deal of discrimination against the residents of Las Yaguas. Their attitude toward society is a reaction against that discrimination. Discrimination still exists; however, now it is not the majority of Cuban society against those who once lived in Las Yaguas, but, rather, it is those who once lived in Las Yaguas against the rest of Cuban society."

What the advisor seemed to be saying was that there was a kind of "reverse discrimination" taking place; or, perhaps more accurately, or prosaically, he meant that the former Las Yaguas dwellers were saying in effect to their fellow Cubans, "It's all well and good that you may now regard us as your equals in some ways. But we don't forget all those years when we were treated like dirt, and we won't let you forget it." As a matter for speculation, it is not inconceivable that the reluctance to elect judges from Buena Ventura may have been a result of some apprehension on the part of their neighbors that Buena Venturans might not be impartial in their judgments involving "outsiders."

In any case, the advisor quoted above believed that there should be more local representation in the courts but thought that the lack of such representation was not an insurmountable or a permanent problem:

> Our job is to bring justice into the heart of these communities so that the people can see it and let it serve as an example, not simply to prevent crimes, but to let the people see that they have the opportunity of incorporating themselves into future tribunals. The People's Courts have not been established once and for all, now and forever. Periodically there are new assemblies which incorporate new members. Those who did not make it the first time may feel rejected, but when they see that the requirements are not that stiff, that you do not have to be a professional but only logical, moral, and revolutionary enough to judge your peers, they will realize that they can become involved at any moment. We all hope for that involvement.

He assumed that increased exposure to People's Courts would allow the people of Buena Ventura to understand its goals. The trials of Jacinto and Panchita, however, seem to indicate that the educational motivation behind the courts was not fully understood in Buena Ventura. And the courts' loosely defined procedures and sanctions, although designed to provide flexible individual judgments and to emphasize rehabilitation, were interpreted by both litigants as capricious and even vindictive. The critical admonitions and the "constructive" sanctions they interpreted as punitive measures, to be forgotten or avoided if possible. After several trials, neither Panchita nor Jacinto had shown any indication of becoming more productive or less alienated citizens. The people of Buena Ventura still, it appears, regarded the courts as "something official, something which comes down from above, something alien to them." an attitude which Blas Roca had hoped the People's Courts would dissolve.[16]

Despite official claims to the contrary, in certain respects the concept held by the people of Buena Ventura about the People's Courts was not totally unwarranted or unrealistic. Although the regional advisor, mentioned above, insisted that discrimination against the former residents of Las Yaguas no longer existed, in practice the judges displayed an attitude which sharply differentiated them from the litigants. Ana Pérez, for example, generalized Panchita's morality to the entire population of Buena Ventura. Another judge who was interviewed described Buena Ventura as "a rat's nest of untrustworthy and immoral people." Still another judge said, "You can put them into a new environment where they are free from previous hostilities and economically better off, and they still maintain the same vices, vicious habits, and other customs. So logically they are going to repeat the same crimes." Such attitudes on the part of the judges have undoubtedly helped to curb the persuasive, egalitarian dialogues that the courts wanted to encourage.

When we left, it was impossible to predict whether the organizers of the People's Courts would attempt to draw more people from Buena Ventura into active participation and control of the courts or simply allow the courts to continue functioning as they had until the people of Buena Ventura were eventually dispersed or gradually changed under the influence of universal free education, guaranteed full employment, improved health service, and other benefits of the new Cuban society. In the meantime, the People's Courts remained an unfinished but nonetheless imaginative and potentially significant experiment in democratic social control.

Notes

1. A "locality" (*localidad*) was an ill-defined administrative or jurisprudential unit which, in the countryside, might be a village or hamlet and in the city a zone comprising several thousand people. Buena Ventura was thus just one of a number of neighborhoods within the jurisdiction of a single court.

2. It is anticipated that the transcripts of the trials will be published and analyzed separately.

3. Tribunales Populares is variously translated as People's Courts, Popular Courts, or Popular Tribunals.

4. J. Berman, "The Cuban Popular Tribunals," *Columbia Law Review* 69, no. 8 (1969):1321–29, lists the cases which, as of 1968, fell within the jurisdiction of the People's Courts. These laws were derived almost entirely from the liberal Social Defense Code (Código de Defensa Social) of 1938 and were the ones in effect at the time of our study. In 1969 the Cuban Judicial Studies Commission (Comisiones de Estudios Judiciales) had begun a plan to reorganize the Cuban legal system. Certain

modifications in the law were institutionalized in July, 1973, including the introduction of nonprofessional judges into the Regional, Provincial, and Supreme courts. See *Granma Weekly Review*, July 15, 1973, pp. 4–5; *Bohemia*, July, August, and September, 1973; and David Booth, "Neighbourhood Committees and Popular Courts in the Social Transformation of Cuba" (Ph.D. diss., University of Surrey, 1973).

5. Booth, "Neighbourhood Committees," pp. 167–68.

6. Cited in Berman, "Cuban Popular Tribunals," p. 1318.

7. Other groups, such as the Young Communists and the Federation of Cuban Women, occasionally submitted lists of candidates.

8. For a discussion of the manual, see Berman, "Cuban Popular Tribunals," pp. 1336–37.

9. A number of other sanctions available to the People's Courts, although they were less frequently imposed, included attendance in literacy classes, prohibitions against appearing in certain places (such as bars, before they were closed down), confinement to residence, and relocation to a new neighborhood (*ibid.*, pp. 1329–32).

10. As of 1973, judges were no longer allowed to conduct such investigations (*Bohemia*, July, 1973, p. 15).

11. Booth, "Neighbourhood Committees," p. 163.

12. Spontaneous testimony was discontinued in 1973 (*Bohemia*, September, 1973, p. 14).

13. Richard R. Fagen, *The Transformation of Political Culture in Cuba*, p. 2.

14. Ernesto Guevara, *Socialism and Man*, p. 7.

15. The names of the judges and litigants are fictitious.

16. Berman, "Cuban Popular Tribunals," p. 1318.

9

Participation in Other Revolutionary Organizations and Programs

The Federation of Cuban Women

The Federación de Mujeres Cubanas (Federation of Cuban Women —FMC) was a mass organization founded in 1960. It was open to all women fifteen years of age and older. Vilma Espín, president and one of the founders of the FMC, described its purpose: "The Federation prepares women educationally, politically, and socially to participate in the Revolution. As an arm of the Revolution, its main functions are the incorporation of women in work and raising the educational level—including political consciousness—of women."[1]

The FMC mobilized women for agriculture and military emergencies, trained them for and tried to place them in new jobs, and engaged them in various other government projects. One of its 'main achievements was its role in helping to establish the *círculos infantiles* and *jardines*.[2] Still, there were problems, not only in Buena Ventura but also nationally, concerning the incorporation of women in the work force. In 1977 Vilma Espín reported that the FMC was "working tenaciously" to improve the cultural level and technical training of young women who are neither working nor studying."[3]

As with other organizations for the masses, membership in the FMC was voluntary, but pressures were brought to bear and incentives established in order to bolster membership. Women generally had to belong to the federation in order to get a job, so women who wanted to work were virtually forced to join the mass organization. In Las Yaguas in 1961 it was rumored (incorrectly) that a woman had to be a member of the FMC to be eligible for a home in one of the new housing settlements. Socorro Bajaraja, a woman of fifty-nine, told us that she enlisted in the FMC because even though she knew nothing about the organization—not even that it was directed by women—she wanted a house in Buena Ventura.

In 1969 only 29 of 105 women between the ages of fifteen and sixty-five in Buena Ventura belonged to the FMC. This relatively low proportion of women in Buena Ventura belonging to the federation (27.6 percent) reflected the small percentage of women in the project who were employed (25.9 percent).

There was widespread complaint by the women of Buena Ventura that the federation was ineffective. Lucía Martínez, for example, had belonged to the FMC since its founding in Las Yaguas. Just as officials of the CDRs had done, following the move to Buena Ventura, officials of the federation generated some enthusiasm among residents of the new housing project. Lucía recalled that FMC meetings were held periodically to organize tasks such as mobilization for agriculture and that the FMC was responsible for installing the bus route which ran through the *reparto*. "But," she said, "now they don't do anything."

A higher-echelon official of the FMC, in turn, expressed dismay at the lack of cooperation and interest by the residents of Buena Ventura. An important problem centered around issuance of FMC membership cards to those who had applied for them. Some women who had applied and who had been paying dues ("voluntary contributions") refused to pay any more until they received their membership cards. Several women we interviewed in Buena Ventura had become frustrated and disheartened at finding a job or even participating in activities such as the mobilizations because they had no identification card.

Compulsory Military Service

Compulsory Military Service (Servicio Militar Obligatorio—SMO) was put into effect in 1963. All men between the ages of sixteen and forty-five were technically eligible to be drafted into the armed forces (usually the army) to complete three years of service.[4] Upon completion of military service, those who did not reenlist entered the organized reserves until they reached their forty-fifth birthday. Apparently few of the older eligible men were drafted, but beginning in 1964, the Compulsory Military Service law was enforced for persons between the ages of sixteen and twenty-two.

In addition to training Cuban youths in military preparedness, one result of enforcement of the SMO law in the age group sixteen to twenty-two was to curtail further rural-urban migration, since it was primarily among this age group that major migration took place.[5] Another consequence of the conscription laws was to keep vagrants off the streets. The draft system was thus a mechanism of political and economic mobilization. It generated a significant amount of cheap labor and was a mechanism of control and surveillance of political dissidents and other "antisocial" types.[6]

In Buena Ventura, eleven young men were doing their military service in 1969–70. They were all between the ages of sixteen and nineteen, had not been attending school at the time of induction, and had been marginally employed or unemployed at that time. Many had reputations as loafers or delinquents.

Two men from Buena Ventura were serving in the standing military force of Cuba in 1969–70. This force, the Fuerzas Armadas Revolucionarias (the Revolutionary Armed Forces—FAR), was composed of those wishing to perform voluntary military service. FAR had perhaps 100,000 to 120,000 men and women in 1969 (figures were kept confidential). These regular forces were supported by a number of paramilitary organizations, the principal one being the Popular Militia. Redesignated the Civil Defense in early 1969, it was estimated to number over 250,000 men and women.[7]

Ejidio Salinas was twenty years old when we interviewed him about his brief stay in the FAR.

> I was fifteen when I signed up, lying about my age in order to get into the Service. That was in 1965, and I had no birth certificate; I didn't get one until later. I entered the Service because I always thought I'd like the army. But as much as I liked it, there were bad things, too. For instance, they were always punishing me by taking away my passes.
>
> I went AWOL once because it had been a long time since I had seen my family. I went home and was there about a month when they caught me. They brought me before a military court. I testified that I had gone because my mother was sick. My mother has some nervous disorder or disease, but they didn't believe me and sentenced me without even trying to verify my story. That was the first time I went AWOL, and I was sentenced to one year on a prison farm.[8]

I think the sanction was just, because, after all, I was the one who had gone AWOL and deserved the punishment. But I think they should have tried to verify my story, to find out if I was lying or telling the truth. But they claimed that so many comrades told the same stories when they ran away that they couldn't possibly investigate them all. Well, all they would have had to do was to visit my house to find out if it was true, but they didn't and punished me anyway.

They sent me from the prison farm to Camagüey, where UMAP is.[9] That was all agricultural work, too. They used to give passes, but they were short, from twelve to twenty-four hours, so you could only go into town. The prison farm was better because it was right here in Havana, while UMAP was clear out in Camagüey.

Life in UMAP was rather hard, and they treated you badly. There was a lieutenant in charge of the unit who was mentally ill. Whenever there were fights or disorders, he ordered the guards to shoot in the air or to prick the prisoners with bayonets. When they fired, it was always in the air, never at anyone. They went at two or three guys with bayonets because there were arguments which ended up in fist fights. They'd strike you or push you down and then go at you with the bayonet. When you see someone wielding a bayonet you get out of there in a hurry. That's how they controlled people there.

Among the things that interested us in Ejidio's narrative was the rather harsh treatment accorded the interns by the UMAP. There have been many reports of this, but few first-hand recorded experiences.[10]

The transfer of Ejidio from regular service duty to a *granja* and then to the UMAP must have been unusual, since prison farms were apparently used mainly for political prisoners.

Mobilization for Agriculture

Cuba was relying heavily on the use of unpaid labor during the time of our study, largely in the attempt to fill the sugar quota. Mesa-Lago distinguished five types of unpaid labor: (1) work performed by employed workers outside of regular working time; (2) work done by unemployed women; (3) work performed by students as a method of socialist education; (4) work accomplished by prisoners as a means of "social rehabilitation"; and (5) work included as part of the compulsory military service.[11] Degrees of pressure to perform voluntary labor ranged from exhortations and emulation (employed workers, unemployed women) to forced labor (military recruits and prison-

ers). Since 1964 mobilization campaigns for labor had been compulsory for students of elementary schools and high schools during
vacation periods.

Unpaid labor performed by employed male and female workers
was usually called "voluntary labor." It was performed beyond regular working hours, either at their work center or some other place.
Voluntary labor could be accomplished in four different ways: as
overtime hours after the regular workday; on weekends, especially on
Sundays; during the annual paid vacation time; and for a continuous
period of several months during leave of absence from a regular job. In
the last, workers left their regular jobs from one to six months to work
mainly in agriculture; they were called *permanentes,* or long-time
volunteers. Because such workers used a leave of absence, they were
paid their regular wages. Their work companions who stayed on the
job site had to maintain production quotas by carrying out the duties
of those mobilized.[12]

To learn the extent to which people in Buena Ventura participated
in voluntary agricultural work, we administered questionnaires to
seventy-five households concerning volunteer work activities of all
able-bodied members of the home between the ages of fourteen and
sixty-five years. The sample contained 159 individuals, 78 men
and 81 women.[13] Of these people, only 62 (38.9 percent) had
ever participated in an agricultural mobilization—47 men and 15
women. Ninety-seven persons (61.1 percent) had never taken part
in a mobilization.

Table 14 is a breakdown of the number of times people in Buena
Ventura had contributed their unpaid labor to agricultural work from
1960 to 1969.[14] As may be seen, the range is from one to nine times
per individual. Only eight people (12.9 percent), all of them men, had
participated on more than three occasions. Seven people had
participated only on Sundays (from one to six times). Five had gone
for up to a period of two weeks at a time, seven for a month, and one
for forty-five days. At the time of our study, five of those who had
been mobilized were performing long-time service in agriculture. Of
the 159 men and women, 33 had at one time or other since 1960 done
long service in agriculture for a period exceeding forty-five days.

Men in all age groups were represented in the mobilization. In
contrast, most of the women (eleven of the fifteen) who had participated were in their teens or early twenties. Thirteen of the fifteen
women were unmarried and/or students.

Table 14. Agricultural Mobilization in Buena Ventura

Number of Mobilizations	Number of Men	Number of Women	Total
1	18	10	28
2	10	3	13
3	11	2	13
4	2	0	2
5	0	0	0
6	2	0	2
7	2	0	2
8	1	0	1
9	1	0	1
Totals	47	15	62

Paula Loredo was a fifteen-year-old student when she volunteered to do agricultural work in 1969. Her comments showed mixed motivations for choosing to work in the countryside: patriotism, a feeling of comradeship, and release from the constraints of family and home life.

I worked in the countryside for thirty-eight days and was happier than I am at home. Just being with the other workers and seeing things that we planted with our own hands grow made me feel good. I felt that I was really doing something for the people. I didn't have to go to the countryside to work, but I wanted to because I've always liked doing voluntary labor. My parents were glad that I went and didn't try to talk me out of it. I learned that a girl is happier when she's working than when she's just sitting around the house doing nothing.

Paula's sister, Lucía, also had a positive reaction to her experience in productive labor: Lucía had attended school at night and worked in a cafeteria during the day until she was put on shift work. She later got dismissed from her job. She told us: "I got laid off in November of 1967. I think it was November fourth. The government closed down the cafeteria because it was privately owned.[15] I went to work in agriculture, at first voluntarily, then they made me go because I was being paid but didn't have a job.[16] People who had been laid off had to go to work in agriculture. I was sent to a place outside of Havana where I planted coffee and spread manure on seedlings. I liked the work. In fact, I liked it better than any other job I've had."

Why did not more residents of Buena Ventura participate in the mobilizations? For one thing, there was no effective recruitment policy or recruiting organization to mobilize them. At the local level, the block CDRs were, as we have shown, almost totally ineffectual, and the sectional CDR had virtually abandoned its responsibilities to the block-level organizations. The last time the sectional office had organized a mobilization for agriculture for the *reparto*, the people who turned out from Buena Ventura were left standing in the cold predawn gray awaiting in vain the arrival of buses to take them to the countryside. The sectional officials later explained that there was no gasoline for the buses, but did not explain why no one had taken the trouble to advise the residents of Buena Ventura of that. Then there were the hazards, particularly to those who were inexperienced in agriculture. Several informants showed us scars from wounds received as a result of their inexperience with cutting cane with a machete. Cristina Ferrer of the housing project left agricultural labor because of accidents involving transport trucks on the job. These dangers, of course, were as much present for other volunteers as they were for the men and women from Buena Ventura; but for a people not used to team effort and not as exposed to government propaganda and exhortations through mass organizations as were many of the others, it may have detracted from their already weak incentive to provide free labor in agriculture.

Finally, the Buena Venturans had more than their share of what Huberman and Sweezy called lack of good work habits. In discussing the trend in Cuba in the late 1960's toward a "semimilitarization" of agriculture, they contended that this trend "has its roots in the necessity to combat one of the most pernicious and at the same time intractable inheritances from the past, the absence of good work habits in a large part of the Cuban population."[17]

Notes

1. Quoted in Elizabeth Sutherland, *The Youngest Revolution*, p. 173.
2. José Moreno, "From Traditional to Modern Values," in *Revolutionary Change in Cuba*, ed. Carmelo Mesa-Lago, p. 481; Sutherland, *Youngest Revolution*, pp. 173–74.
3. *Granma Weekly Review*, September 4, 1977, p. 1.
4. Students could perform their service at their educational institutes. According to law, women were also eligible to be conscripted, but, insofar as we knew, a woman had never been drafted.
5. Nelson Amaro and Carmelo Mesa-Lago, "Inequality and Classes," in *Revolutionary Change in Cuba*, ed. Carmelo Mesa-Lago, p. 344.
6. James M. Malloy, "Generation of Political Support and Allocation of Costs," in *Revolutionary Change in Cuba*, ed. Carmelo Mesa-Lago, p. 36.
7. Howard I. Blutstein et al., *Area Handbook for Cuba*, p. 439.
8. Prison farms (*granjas*) were designed to "reeducate" prisoners who had already served time in jail and who were considered suitable for more advanced rehabilitation.

The *granja* prisoners usually spent part of the day in school and part in the fields (Lee Lockwood, *Castro's Cuba; Cuba's Fidel,* p. 249).

9. Unidades Militares para Ayudar la Producción (Military Units to Aid Production).

10. Cf. José Yglesias, *In the Fist of the Revolution: Life in a Cuban Country Town,* pp. 274–303.

11. Carmelo Mesa-Lago, "Economic Significance of Unpaid Labor in Socialist Cuba," *Industrial and Labor Relations Review* 22, no. 3 (1969):340. Prisoners in work camps were paid for their labor.

12. *Ibid.,* p. 341.

13. Young men doing their obligatory military service were exempted from the survey, since they were required to engage in agricultural labor. Handicapped individuals and primary school children were also excluded.

14. The table includes long-term volunteers receiving wages.

15. This would have been some four months before the announcement of the Revolutionary Offensive, indicating (if Lucía is correct in her date) that the government was already taking steps to close down small, privately owned businesses toward the end of 1967.

16. Employees who were laid off because their place of employment was closed down or because of excess workers continued to receive their wages.

17. Leo Huberman and Paul M. Sweezy, *Socialism in Cuba,* p. 149.

Concluding Remarks

Ten years after the triumph of the Revolution, and despite major efforts by the Castro government to reeducate and indoctrinate the people of Buena Ventura, most of the former Las Yaguas families had not lived up to the ideals of the Revolution. Lee Rainwater observed that "if culture is an adaptation to life situations, and if it is transmitted as the accumulated knowledge of the group about how to behave in those situations, and if that knowledge is systematically reinforced by the experience of individuals as they grow up and go about their daily lives, then one can predict that any effort to change culture directly by outside educational intervention is doomed to failure. People have no incentive to change their culture, indeed they would suffer if they tried, unless there is some significant change in their situation."[1]

There was most assuredly a change in the situation of the former Las Yaguans. They had tangible results from the Revolution: secure jobs, a sufficient and balanced diet, excellent health care, and improved housing. It is problematic, even a bit hazardous, to talk about changes in world view, thought ways, values, and life styles of people in the housing project. External conditions imposed by the Revolution did bring about behavior changes among the populace. The CDRs and the FMC tried to enforce school attendance. Work centers attempted to curtail absenteeism and develop good work habits. Irregular survival activities—bottle selling, lottery ticket vending, peddling, and begging—had virtually disappeared in the housing project. Local and national agencies and organizations tried to eliminate or reduce violence, crime, and delinquency in Buena Ventura, and they had, to a large extent, succeeded. But, of course, behavioral changes may not reflect attitudinal changes.

For the people of Buena Ventura (and for most Cubans) there was probably little change in the most fundamental values—race, sex, family life, and so forth. But their perspectives did change. Informants frequently referred to Cuba's international obligations, its place in the world community, and its relationship to the USSR, China, Africa, the United States, and other Latin American nations. They discussed the need to make sacrifices in consumer goods to pay for imports of capital goods and talked about problems of national economy, foreign policy, and the like. This kind of talk may not signal any profound changes, but it certainly says something about a changed world view.

Insofar as "thought ways" are concerned, socialist ideology may give people a whole new set of standards of behavior and interpersonal relationships and a new set of rationales. Even if people's behavior did not change profoundly (and certainly in Buena Ventura it often did not), they had to find new explanations to justify their behavior, their attitudes toward others, and their relation to the larger society.

Basically, it was the youth to which the Revolution looks for its New Men. There was, from the government's point of view during our stay in Cuba, some cause for optimism insofar as Buena Ventura goes, but more cause for concern. There were too many school dropouts, too many loafers, too few who really understood what the Revolution was all about. Educational programs were undoubtedly the best way to imbue youth with the ideals of the Revolution, but many young people saw school, especially boarding school on scholarships, as a means to escape from household responsibilities and family problems.

Finally, let us return to the problem of government-built housing for the poor. We do not know which, if any, alternatives to the relocation of Las Yaguas families *in toto* to new housing in middle-class neighborhoods were put forth by the Cuban government planners. Although Fidel Castro admonished Buena Ventura's neighbors for their complaints about the new housing program with his remark, "If you don't like them, find some place else to live," I wonder if he and his aides took into account the possible feelings of inferiority of the "people down below?"[2]

On the other hand, did they think that dispersing the Las Yaguas families, particularly "problem" families, into a housing project with "socially balanced" or "socially healthy" families was not a viable alternative? Experience in other countries shows that such a procedure may be more efficacious than the one followed by the Cuban government. Fuerst discussed an experiment in handling "socially unbalanced" families in Holland over a forty-year period. The families were first located in segregated "camps" where they were given intensive social service assistance in employment, schooling, homemaker service, and other needs. At the same time, six housing projects containing a maximum of two hundred units each were constructed in which only those families with serious social problems were located. The projects ranged from those that provided massive social services to those that contained no such services at all.

Experience proved that without heavy reliance on social services, the project conditions and occupants' attitudes deteriorated rapidly. Where social services were available, projects remained adequate in physical facilities, and some families showed sociopsychological improvement. The Dutch government eventually concluded that such projects segregated occupants too sharply from the larger community, and the costs were greater than the advantages obtained. As of 1974, the Dutch government was no longer building such projects but instead was building moderately large public housing projects which included a controlled percentage of families with serious problems. In contact with functioning families, plus outside services, these families improve their social situation somewhat more effectively.[3]

In the case of Cuba, if it had become clear that it was a mistake to have relocated the families from Las Yaguas in the manner chosen, about the only thing the government could have done would have been to shift numbers of former slum dwellers out of Buena Ventura into middle-class neighborhoods and to replace them with residents from the latter. I doubt that this plan would have been any more successful than the original one. In 1969–70 urban construction in Cuba was at a premium, so new "integrated" housing developments were out of the question. Furthermore, provision of more services—the felt needs discussed in chapter 2—was unlikely for years to come because of the shortage of materials and manpower.

It is hoped that reestablishment of good relations and communications between the United States and Cuba will allow us to find out more about the recent past, the present, and the future of the residents of Buena Ventura.

Notes

1. Lee Rainwater, *Behind Ghetto Walls: Black Families in a Federal Slum*, p. 401.

2. Rainwater notes "the apparent inability of public institutions to change in ways that allow them to serve lower-class populations without also demeaning them, or to

obligate the tremendous resources that would be necessary to carry out culture change or opportunity programs that might prove effective" (*ibid.*, p. 401).

3. J. S. Fuerst, ed., *Public Housing in Europe and America*, p. 180. Fuerst infers from this experience that a project can absorb only 2 or 3 percent of the socially unbalanced before the project becomes unacceptable to low-and middle-income families striving for upward mobility. Holland recognized that socially unbalanced families can be divided into those who can benefit from treatment and services and those who cannot. Furthermore, it is learned that placing a large number of such families in the projects does nothing for such families and lowers the living standard for the remainder of the project inhabitants.

Bibliography

Abrams, Charles.
    1964.   *Man's Struggle for Shelter in an Urbanizing World*. Cambridge, Mass.: The M.I.T. Press.

Acosta, Maruja, and Jorge E. Hardoy.
    1973.   *Urban Reform in Revolutionary Cuba*, trans. Mal Bochner. New Haven: Antilles Research Program Occasional Papers No. 1.

Allardt, Erik.
    1973.   Revolutionary Ideologies as Agents of Cultural Change. In *Social Science and the New Societies: Problems in Cross-Cultural Research and Theory Building,* ed. Nancy Hammond. East Lansing, Mich.: Social Science Research Bureau, Michigan State University.

Ames, David W.
    1950.   Negro Family Types in a Cuban Solar. *Phylon* 11(2):159–63.

Bascom, William R.
    1950.   The Focus of Cuban Santería. *Southwestern Journal of Anthropology* 6(1):64–68.
    1972.   *Shangó in the New World*. African and Afro-American Research Institute Occasional Publication. Austin: University of Texas Press.

Bastide, Roger.
    1969.   *Las Américas negras: Las civilizaciones africanas en el Nuevo Mundo*. Madrid: Alianza Editorial.

Berman, J.
    1969.   The Cuban Popular Tribunals. *Columbia Law Review* 69(8):1317–54.

Bernal, J. D.
    1939.   *The Social Function of Science*. London: George Routledge & Sons.
Blutstein, Howard I., et al.
    1971.   *Area Handbook for Cuba*. Washington, D.C.: Government Printing Office.
Bohemia
    1968.   July 5 (suppl.):112.
    1970*a*.   March 27(13):64–65.
    1970*b*.   June 26(26):68.
    1973*a*.   July '(29):72–73.
    1973*b*.   August (33):48–49.
    1973*c*.   September (38):14–15.
Boorstein, Edward.
    1968.   *The Economic Transformation of Cuba*. New York: Monthly Review Press.
Booth, David.
    1973.   Neighbourhood Committees and Popular Courts in the Social Transformation of Cuba. Ph.D. diss., University of Surrey.
Bott, Elizabeth.
    1957.   *Family and Social Network*. London: Tavistock.
Butterworth, Douglas.
    1974.   Grass-roots Political Organization in Cuba: A Case of the Committees for the Defense of the Revolution. In *Latin American Urban Research:* Anthropological Perspectives on Latin American Urbanization, vol. IV, ed. Wayne A. Cornelius and Felicity Trueblood. Beverly Hills: Sage Publications
Castro, Fidel.
    1962.   Mesa redonda sobre reforma urbana. *Obra Revolucionaria*, June 5, p. 6.
    1968   *Discursos de Fidel en los aniversarios de los CDR 1960–1967*. Havana: Instituto del Libro.
    1969.   *History Will Absolve Me*. Havana: Instituto del Libro, Editorial de Ciencias Sociales.
Chailloux Cardona, Juan M.
    1945.   *Síntesis histórica de la vivienda popular: los horrores del solar habanero*. Havana: Biblioteca de Historia, Filosofía y Sociología.
Commission on Cuban Affairs.
    1935.   *Problems of the New Cuba: Report of the Commission on Cuban Affairs*. New York: Foreign Policy Association.

Con la Guardia en Alto.
    1976.   Vol. 15(3).
Cuba, Dirección Nacional de los CDR.
    1965*a*.   *Pueblo organizado.* Havana: Ediciones con la Guardia en Alto.
    1965*b*.   *Los CDR en granjas y zonas rurales.* Havana: Ediciones con la Guardia en Alto.
Cuba, El Movimiento Educativo 1967–68.
    1968.   *Informe a la XXXI Conferencia Internacional de Instrucción pública convocada por la OIE y la UNESCO.* Havana: Instituto del Libro.
Cuba, Instituto Nacional de Reforma Agraria.
    1960.   *Ley de Reforma Agraria.* Havana.
Cuban Economic Research Project.
    1965.   *A Study on Cuba.* Coral Gables; Fla.: University of Miami Press.
Cuba Review.
    1975.   March.
Dimaio, Alfred John, Jr.
    1974.   *Soviet Urban Housing: Problems and Policies.* New York: Praeger.
Direct from Cuba
    n.d.   *Committees for the Defense of the Revolution.*
Dumont, Rene.
    1970.   *Cuba: Socialism and Development.* New York: Grove Press, Inc.
Eames, Edwin, and Judith Granich Goode.
    1977.   *Anthropology of the City: An Introduction to Urban Anthropology.* Englewood Cliffs, N.J.: Prentice-Hall.
Fagen, Richard R.
    1969.   *The Transformation of Political Culture in Cuba.* Stanford: Stanford University Press.
Ford, James A.
    1954.   On the Concept of Types: The Type Concept Revisited. *American Anthropologist* 56(1): 42–54.
Foreign Policy Association.
    1935.   *Problems of the New Cuba.* New York: Foreign Policy Association.
Fried, Marc.
    1963.   Grieving for a Lost Home. In *The Urban Condition: People and Policy in the Metropolis,* ed. Leonard J. Duhl. New York: Basic Books.

Fried, Marc, and Peggy Gleicher.
1961.   Some Sources of Residential Satisfaction in an Urban Slum. *American Institute of Planners* 27(4):305–15.
Fuerst, J. S., ed.
1974.   *Public Housing in Europe and America.* New York: John Wiley & Sons.
Gans, Herbert J.
1965.   *The Urban Villagers: Group and Class in the Life of Italian-Americans.* New York: The Free Press.
García Alonso, Aida.
1968.   *Manuela la Mexicana.* Havana: Casa de las Américas.
Garnier, Jean-Pierre.
1973.   *Une ville, une révolution: La Havane, de l'urbain au politique.* Paris: Editions Anthropos.
Gluckman, Max.
1963.   Gossip and Scandal. *Current Anthropology* 4(3):307–13.
Goffman, Erving.
1963.   *Stigma: Notes on the Management of Spoiled Identity.* Englewood Cliffs, N.J.: Prentice-Hall.
González, Nancie L. Solien.
1969.   *Black Carib Household Structure.* Seattle: University of Washington Press.
1970.   Toward a Definition of Matrifocality. In *Afro-American Anthropology: Contemporary Perspectives*, ed. Norman E. Whitten, Jr., and John F. Szwed. New York: The Free Press.
Granma.
1969.   January 20; July 4.
1970.   May 13; August 23.
1972.   October 8.
Granma Weekly Review.
1969.   August 31.
1970.   January 25.
1971.   March 28; May 9.
1973.   April 29; July 15.
1977.   September 4; October 2; October 9.
Guevara, Ernesto.
1969.   *Socialism and Man.* New York: Young Socialist Alliance.
Hart, Armando.
1963.   Educational Progress in New Cuba. *Political Affairs* 42(5):38–46.
Hartman, Chester.
1963a.   The Limitations of Public Housing. *American Institute of Planners Journal* 29:283–96.

1963*b*.   Social Values and Housing Orientations. *Journal of Social Issues* 19(2):113–31.

1966.   *Family Turnover in Public Housing*. San Juan, Puerto Rico: Urban Renewal and Housing Administration.

Hernández, Roberto E., and Carmelo Mesa-Lago.

1971.   Labor Organization and Wages. Revolutionary Change in Cuba, ed. Carmelo Mesa-Lago. Pittsburgh: University of Pittsburgh Press.

Huberman, Leo, and Paul M. Sweezy.

1969.   *Socialism in Cuba*. New York: Monthly Review Press.

Jahn, Jahnheinz.

1966.   *Muntu: An Outline of New African Culture*. New York: Grove Press.

Jolly, Richard.

1964.   Education. In *Cuba: The Economic and Social Revolution*, ed. Dudley Sears. Durham: The University of North Carolina Press.

Karol, K. S.

1970.   *Guerrillas in Power: The Course of the Cuban Revolution*. New York: Hill and Wang.

Kenner, Martin, and James Petras, eds.

1969.   *Fidel Castro Speaks*. New York: Grove Press.

Lachatañere, Romulo.

1942.   *Manual de santería*. Estudios afro-cubanos. Havana: Editorial Caribe.

Leiner, Marvin, with Robert Ubell.

1974.   *Children Are the Revolution: Day Care in Cuba*. New York: Viking Press.

Lewis, Gordon K.

1963.   *Puerto Rico: Freedom and Power in the Caribbean*. New York: Monthly Review Press.

Lewis, Oscar

1951.   *Life in a Mexican Village: Tepoztlán Revisited*. Urbana, Illinois, University of Illinois Press.

1952.   Urbanization without breakdown: a case study. *Scientific Monthly* 75 (1):31–4.

1958.   The Culture of the Vecindad in Mexico City: Two Case Studies. In *Actas del XXXIII Congreso Internacional de Americanistas*. San José, Costa Rica: Congreso Internacional de Americanistas.

1963.   The Culture of Poverty. *Trans-Action* 1(1):17–22.

1966a.   Even the Saints Cry. *Trans-Action* 4(1):8–23.

1966b.   *La Vida. A Puerto Rican Family in the Culture of Poverty*

—*San Juan and New York.* New York: Random House.

Lewis, Oscar, with the assistance of Douglas Butterworth.
1968.   *A Study of Slum Culture: Backgrounds for La Vida.* New York: Random House.

Lewis, Oscar, Ruth M Lewis, and Susan M. Rigdon.
1977.   *Four Men: Living the Revolution: An Oral History of Contemporary Cuba.* Urbana: University of Illinois Press.
1977.   *Four Women: Living the Revolution: An Oral History of Contemporary Cuba.* Urbana: University of Illinois Press.
1978.   *Neighbors: Living the Revolution: An Oral History of Contemporary Cuba.* Urbana: University of Illinois Press.

Lockwood, Lee.
1969.   *Castro's Cuba: Cuba's Fidel.* New York: Vintage Books.

Loney, Martin.
1973.   Social Control in Cuba. In *Politics and Deviance,* ed. Ian Taylor and Laurie Taylor. Hammondsworth, England: Penguin.

MacGaffey, Wyatt, and Clifford R. Barnett.
1962.   *Cuba: Its People, Its Society, Its Culture.* New Haven: HRAF Press.
1965.   *Twentieth-Century Cuba: The Background of the Castro Revolution.* Garden City, N.Y.: Anchor Books.

Malloy, James M.
1971.   Generation of Political Support and Allocation of Costs. In *Revolutionary Change in Cuba,* ed. Carmelo Mesa-Lago. Pittsburgh: University of Pittsburgh Press.

Mangin, William.
1967.   Latin American Squatter Settlements: A Problem and a Solution. *Latin American Research Review* 2(3):65–98.

Martínez-Alier, Verena.
1974.   *Marriage, Class and Colour in Nineteenth-Century Cuba.* Cambridge: Cambridge University Press.

Mesa-Lago, Carmelo.
1969.   Economic Significance of Unpaid Labor in Socialist Cuba. *Industrial and Labor Relations Review* 22(3):339–57.

Mesa-Lago, Carmelo, ed.
1971.   *Revolutionary Change in Cuba.* Pittsburgh: University of Pittsburgh Press.

Mesa-Lago, Carmelo, and Luc Zephirin.
1971.   Central Planning. In *Revolutionary Change in Cuba,* ed. Carmelo Mesa-Lago. Pittsburgh: University of Pittsburgh Press.

Moreno, José A.
    1971.   From Traditional to Modern Values. In *Revolutionary Change in Cuba,* ed. Carmelo Mesa-Lago. Pittsburgh: University of Pittsburgh Press.
Morgan, Ted.
    1974.   Cubans' Love Story with Castro Continues. *Chicago Sun-Times,* Dec. 16, p. 2.
Nelson, Lowry.
    1950.   *Rural Cuba.* Minneapolis: University of Minnesota Press.
    1972.   *Cuba: Measure of a Revolution.* Minneapolis: University of Minnesota Press.
New York Times.
    1944.   Article, p. 19.
    1961   Castro's Repressive Acts Awaken Cubans to Reality. June 12, p. 1; June 13, p. 18.
New York Times Magazine.
    1961.   Case Study of a Police State. April 30, p. 88.
Obra Revolucionaria.
    1962.   No. 7 (March 14).
O'Connor, James.
    1970.   *The Origins of Socialism in Cuba.* Ithaca, N.Y.: Cornell University Press.
Parker, Seymour, and Robert J. Kleiner.
    1970.   The Culture of Poverty: An Adjustive Dimension. *American Anthropologist* 72(3): 516–27.
Parsons, Elsie Clews.
    1936.   *Mitla, Town of Souls.* Chicago: University of Chicago Press.
Phillips, Ruby Hart.
    1962.   *Cuba: Island of Paradox.* New York: McDowell, Obolensky.
Rabkin, Yakov M.
    1977.   Review of *Soviet Sociology of Science* by Linda L. Lubrano. *Science* 197 (August): 856–57.
Rainwater, Lee.
    1970.   *Behind Ghetto Walls: Black Families in a Federal Slum.* Chicago: Aldine.
Revolución.
    1961.   April 24.
Rodman, Hyman.
    1971.   *Lower-Class Families: The Culture of Poverty in Negro Trinidad.* New York: Oxford University Press.
Safa, Helen Icken.

1974.   *The Urban Poor of Puerto Rico: A Study in Development and Inequality.* New York: Holt, Rinehart and Winston.

Seers, Dudley, et al.
1964.   *Cuba: The Economic and Social Revolution.* Chapel Hill: University of North Carolina Press.

Smith, M. G.
1962.   *West Indian Family Structure.* Seattle: University of Washington Press.

Smith, Raymond T.
1956.   *The Negro Family in British Guiana.* London: Routledge & Kegan Paul.
1960.   The Family in the Caribbean. In *Caribbean Studies: A Symposium,* ed. Vera Rubin. Seattle: University of Washington Press.
1963.   Culture and Social Structure in the Caribbean: Some Recent Work on Family and Kinship Studies. *Comparative Studies in Society and History* 6:24–46.

Smith, Robert Freeman.
1966.   *Background to Revolution: The Development of Modern Cuba.* New York: Alfred A. Knopf.

Steward, Julian H.
1954.   On the Concept of Types: Types of Types. *American Anthropologist* 56(1):54–57.

Sutherland, Elizabeth.
1969.   *The Youngest Revolution.* New York: Dial Press.

Suttles, Gerald D.
1972.   *The Social Construct of Communities.* Chicago: University of Chicago Press.

Thomas, Hugh.
1971.   *Cuba: The Pursuit of Freedom.* New York: Harper & Row.

Turner, John C.
1967.   Barriers and Channels for Housing Development in Modernizing Countries. *Journal of the American Institute of Planners* 33:167–81.

U.S., Department of Labor, Office of Policy Planning and Research.
1965.   *The Negro Family: The Case for National Action.* Washington, D.C.: Government Printing Office.

Valdés, Nelson P.
1972.   The Radical Transformation of Cuban Education. In *Cuba in Revolution,* ed. Rolando E. Bonachea and Nelson P. Valdés. New York: Anchor Books.

Valentine, Charles A.
1968.   *Culture and Poverty: Critique and Counter-Proposals.* Chicago: University of Chicago Press.

Wall Street Journal.
  1970. Comrade Spy: How a Cuban Worker Helps Keep "Revolution" Alive. August 20, pp. 1, 15.

Wolf, Eric R.
  1969. *Peasant Wars of the Twentieth Century.* New York: Harper and Row.

Yglesias, José.
  1968. *In the Fist of the Revolution: Life in a Cuban Country Town.* New York: Random House.

Index

Abortions, 90–91
Agricultural mobilization, 106, 136–38, 139n13
—problems, 137–38
Alienation, sense of, 26–27, 68
Attitudes, in Buena Ventura: changes, post-Revolution, 141; on education, 96; on sex, 79–81, 91n5; toward one another, 29, 77–79, 81–82, 115, 128; toward People's Courts, 129; toward rationing, 38

Bay of Pigs invasion: Cuban reactions, 85, 106, 107, 108, 116n8
Black market, small scale, 38, 40
Buena Ventura. *See* specific subject headings

Castro, Fidel: and the Oscar Lewis Cuba Project, xii–xiii; Great Revolutionary Offensive, 31; "History Will Absolve Me" speech, 18; offensive against illiteracy, 98; on crime, 117n25; on housing complaints, 141; on premarital sex, 53; on system of collective vigilance, 106, 116n1; suspension of the Cuba Project, xxi; Twenty-sixth of July Movement, xiv
Census, Cuban, 24–25, 108
Children, changes in lifestyle of, 35, 58
Committees for the Defense of the Revolution (CDRs): cadre schools, 108; court duties, 109; guard duty, 109, 112, 113; member's duties, 100, 106, 108–10; organization of, 110–11;

organization of, in Buena Ventura, 111–13; problems, 114–116, 117n33, 118n37; recruiting, 105–6, 111, 112; scholars' reactions to, 106–7; sectional committees, 110, 114–115; sectional committees in Buena Ventura, 111–14; vigilance duties, 106, 107, 110, 112
Community services: felt lacking, 26, 30n14; in Buena Ventura, 21, 22, 25, 26; in Las Yaguas, 6–7
Confederation of Cuban Workers, 37
Conflicts between families: in Buena Ventura, 60–61, 62–64, 76–77, 83; in Las Yaguas, 9–10
Conflicts between neighbors, 74–76, 77, 113
Cordón de la Habana, 45n5
Counterrevolutionaries, xix, 107–8
Crime, 82–84, 91n6, 110, 140
Culture of poverty, xxii–xxvi, xxixn26; in Cuba, xiii, xxi; in Las Yaguas, xxvi; in socialist countries, xiii; inutility in Buena Ventura study, xxvi–xxvii

Defended neighborhoods, 67
Discrimination, neighborhoods of origin: in Buena Ventura, 25, 27–29, 77, 99, 114–15, 127–28, 130; in Las Yaguas, 12, 67
Discrimination, racial: in Buena Ventura, 28, 53, 54, 96; in Las Yaguas, 12
Disease and curing, 89–90
Divorce (marital shifting), 59, 70n3
Drinking, 84
Drugs, 81, 84

Rationing books, xvii, 51, 108
Recycling projects, 109, 113
Religion: Catholicism, 85; *santería*, 16*n*17, 86–89, 92*n*18, 92*n*20; suppression of, 85
Research assistants (*equipo*), xv–xvi, xviii
Revolutionary government, reactions to: in Buena Ventura, 105–6; in Cuba, xiv, xxviii*n*11; in Las Yaguas, 19–20
Revolutionary Offensive, 139*n*15

Sexual activity in Buena Ventura, 52–53, 57
Slum settlements: attempts to expel squatters, 12–14; in Cuba, 3–5; Las Yaguas, 5–6

Social Defense Code, 127, 130*n*4
Social structure. *See* Households
Spontaneous testimony, at trials, 123, 131*n*12
Study circles, 122

Unity: in Las Yaguas, 68–69; lack of in Buena Ventura, 67–68

Voluntary labor, 109, 113, 117*n*20, 135, 136
Vanguard workers, 109

Wages: after Revolution, 40–41, 139*n*16
Work centers, 109, 117*n*19